GRABOVOI GRIGORI

EAM Publishing
Edilma Angel Moyano
Contract: P527USA
That grants the right to use the brands GRABOVOI®
GRIGORI GRABOVOI®, for editions

Copyright © 2022 Dr. Grigori Grabovoi®
ISBN – 9798438523017

TRANSLATED from Russian to English
BY MARIA BARAJAS, AP, RN, BSN, MS Oriental Medicine

Carátula © D'har Services Editorial

Art Cover and Photography © Edilma Angel

Photo DT: 52751730 © Vs1489

THE WORK "NUMBERS FOR SUCCESSFUL BUSINESS" IS CREATED IN
RUSSIAN BY GRIGORI GRABOVOI IN 2004

NUMBERS FOR SUCCESSFUL BUSINESS

A total compilation of numerical series for commercial use

Contents

INTRODUCTION

The work gives numerical series, which by using them in accordance with the terms, definitions and concepts in business, you can successfully develop your own business based on the technologies of eternal development.

Before the action in any area of commodity-money relations, even in the cases when they do not relate to business, you can mentally pronounce the following number series that implements eternal development through the economic sphere: **289 471 314917**

Numerical series implement the solution of the problem of the best, optimal, more efficient use of limited, often rare, resources of economic activity and the management of this process to achieve the goal of maximum satisfaction of the growing and unlimited needs of man and society with eternal development. The numbers for successful business given in this book can be applied to control the economy.

The economy is considered as all kinds of activities of people, human society as a whole, which allow people and society to supply themselves with material resources for life. At the same time, the economy of eternal development is aimed primarily at the reproduction of resources that are not renewable by natural means and are necessary for eternal development. Then the economy of eternal development determines the need to obtain funds for the sphere of life restored and created by natural, social, technologic methods. Man is the basis for the implementation of such an economy. Since the ideas and practical actions of people aimed at eternal development create the economic structure of a society of eternal development.

The totality of human needs is extremely wide, numerous, constantly growing, and becoming more complex. In the economy of perpetual development, it is important, in accordance with the goal, to develop ways of satisfying needs in a creative and reproducible way. Thus, an indisputable fact is considered - the boundlessness and constancy of the growth of human needs.

For business success, it is advisable to read the book in its entirety with the mental pronunciation of the number series. In some cases, the reception of perception is effective, expressed in the fact that you perceive an echo from mentally pronounced numerical series. Echo in the collective consciousness refers to the consequence of current events with sound, that is, it is perceived as an element of a future event. Applying this, one can try to build a control forecast of events in the economic sphere, using numerical series corresponding to terms and concepts. To do this, before starting the mental pronunciation of the series, «sub vocal» pronounce the numbers **889491** and then mentally pronounce the numbers of the series. At the moment of pronouncing the numbers, you can apply the number **91688,** which controls towards the norm of eternal development, if you feel resistance.

Gaps in the series related to the economy of eternal development, along with the numbers of the series, can be perceived as areas of receipt of the money and other resources necessary to ensure eternal life. In this case, the control information from the space has a more generalized character. Conceptually, this information means that in the economy the internal space not filled with information can always be filled with data for eternal development.

If, when pronouncing a row corresponding to a term or concept, a light blue color is perceived, then the situation can be corrected at the speed of real-time control. When perceiving shades of dark colors, it is better to devote time to additional event management. Over time, one can learn to perceive any details of information that causes unnecessary situations, and, as far as possible, correct in advance to the norm. In technologies of eternal development, the main thing is to be able to provide the main platform necessary for eternal life, and in this case, control to the norm must be achieved.

When using numbers to improve business efficiency, you can mentally create control geometric images built in the form of mental images of real events. That is, you can, for example, symbolically represent an enterprise, circulation of documents, cash, a specific document of interest to you or a specific event. Then, mentally moving these objects in the control space of thinking, you need to achieve the desired result. You can also mentally connect the represented objects with light rays, mentally move the object higher if you need to get more information about the object. With a certain practice, it is enough to simply represent the space of one's thinking in the same way as an object in this method of control. Thus, you will be able to improve your thinking by working with the space of thinking. Such practice is useful for rejuvenation in eternal life and increasing the efficiency of thinking through self-government. Since with such a method of action in the control of thinking, one can apply spiritual action. A spiritualized thought can more effectively implement the practice of eternal development.

Since a thought can be perceived verbally, the word spoken from such a thought has the same level of eternity as the spirit, due to the fact that it has the property of self-creation. This means that by mentally pronouncing a word thus prepared, one can reach eternity in those events to which this word or sentences composed of such words relate. It is possible to apply such inspired words before each action in the field of economics and in other fields for the realization of your eternal life and all others. Establishing the reality of eternal life happens faster for everyone when you bring the effect of the spiritualized word on yourself. By managing with the help of numbers from the field of thinking that creates a spiritualized word, you significantly increase the effectiveness of business in the field of eternal development.

In cases where your actions in any economic area, including business, relate to the terms or concepts described in this book, you can mentally pronounce the numbers of the series related to these terms or concepts before starting actions. Apply them when considering any economic question.

Using this method, you will eventually learn to evaluate the mass value of the described numbers, because you can evaluate the mass of the objects around you. Intuitive thinking, on which success in business often depends, in this method will be systemic, which for business means precise. Since intuition in this method functions on the basis of specific numerical masses, that is, according to the laws of the logic of cause-and-effect events. Considering that intuition in business, in fact, is a form of managing largely random events of the future, the method is being transformed into a way to control random events through logic. This is very important, since when realizing eternal development, the logically set task of eternal life must necessarily be accomplished with an infinite number of random events in the future.

The numbers given in the work, in certain cases, are described according to the methodology of their application. If numbers are found after a sentence, term or concept without a description, then all the ways in which they are used in the book apply to them. In this case, the use of numbers means that the definition or event recorded in the sentence, term or concept by means of a number series is brought into the area of the norm for creating the desired event.

Numbers can be viewed as forming elements of goods and services. Then, imagining, for example, a new model of a car consisting of numbers at the level of thinking, one can learn at the level of spirit to determine the defects of the car and its prospects for business. The same applies to all other areas of business. In this method, the numerical series corresponding to the term, concept, event or area of business, in fact, control the indicated masses of numbers in the direction of eternal development.

It is possible, perceiving numbers, to find shades of white in them, through which you can spread the light of your consciousness to the area of business projects. The creators of the action are that by perceiving already different color characteristics of the light of your consciousness, you can understand the deep meaning of a business project that takes into account the methodology of eternal development in the systemic connections of the whole world. Understanding this accelerates the implementation of your business plans.

Before starting any action, you can mentally pronounce the first three numbers of series **419,** implying at the level of consciousness that behind these three numbers there are other numbers, using which you achieve eternal development. At the spiritual level of management, when applying this series, information is created that in general all numbers and any combination of numbers are aimed at eternal development.

From this spiritual state, you are moving with your consciousness into the area of your perception, which contains knowledge of how already from the objects of physical and spiritual reality, by analogy with the use of numbers for eternal development, you can select areas of knowledge and action for your eternal development. Using these areas, you understand that eternal life is a reality created by human activity, taking into account data about the world around him. For the non-dying of another person, you can change the same series with the addition of seven numbers **2890618** after the series.

That is, mentally say the number series: **419 318 88941898 2890618** for the purpose of continuing life of another person.

Business processes use definitions that can be applied in the following ways to ensure perpetuity. eternal development in case of deviation from the norm. Aims at achieving a successful business of eternal development in other cases.

Labor is the expenditure by a person for creative purposes of his physical, intellectual and spiritual energy. Labor in the process of production is characterized by intensity and productivity. Numerical series of restoration of such energy: **8918 014 915 6481**

The intensity of labor is its intensity, measured by the degree of expenditure of labor power per unit of time. The provision of labor productivity necessary for the eternal life of people is determined by the following series: **319 814**

Intensity of labor is its tension estimated in extends of spending of labor force per unit time. Series of increasing of labor intensity with simultaneous recovery of employee health ample for their eternal life is as follows: **814 31989046718911481**

The series of increasing the intensity of labor with the simultaneous restoration of the health of workers sufficient for their eternal life is as follows**: 419 318 88941898** It is important to consider that this series refers not only to labor in production, but in general to any human activity.

Land is a natural resource. The protection of the Earth and the restoration and increase of natural resources in the process of eternal development can be carried out by education, the development of such a state of mind in which it is realized with control methods that physical presence on Earth should be accompanied by care for the Earth. The number series for this is as follows: **914712 819 19 84**

At the same time, it is necessary to be aware that it also refers to protection of the earth from external threat of outer space. Such spirit condition has straight controlled action towards ensuring eternity of the earth simultaneously with eternity of human, and it organizes people to fulfill the tasks of eternal development in all fields of their physical and spiritual activity. In general, in eternal development, the ensuring of eternity of existence natural and artificially produced subjects of outer space through the use of which eternal life of people is being implemented, - this is also the corresponding level of spiritual development.

Capital is the means of production created by people and the money used in the production of goods and services. For the development and increase of capital in the implementation of eternal life, the following number series is applicable: **819048 714 391**

It can be used in analytical work, before specific transactions and other events related to capital. Entrepreneurship is an activity aimed at generating income, profit. In the system of eternal development, the receipt of income is accompanied by the distribution of its part for the implementation of methods and ways of eternal life.

Entrepreneurial activity is expressed in the organization of production in accordance with the goals. The digital series of successful entrepreneurial activity for eternal development is **917 498 814316**

At the same time, one must be aware also about protecting the Earth from external threats from outer space. Such a spiritual state has a direct control effect in the direction of ensuring the eternity of the Earth simultaneously with the eternity of man and organizes people to fulfill the tasks of eternal development in all areas of their physical and spiritual activity. Generally speaking, with eternal development, ensuring the eternity of the existence of natural and artificially created objects for outer space, with the use of which the eternal life of a person is realized, is also an appropriate level of spiritual development.

Capital is the means of production created by people and the money used in the production of goods and services. For the development and increase of capital in the implementation of eternal life, the following number series is applicable: **819048 714 391**

It can be used in analytical work, before specific transactions and other events related to capital. Entrepreneurship is an activity aimed at generating income, profit. In the system of eternal development, the receipt of income is accompanied by the distribution of its part for the implementation of methods and ways of eternal life. Entrepreneurial activity is expressed in the organization of production in accordance with the goals. The digital series of successful entrepreneurial activity for eternal development is **917 498 814316**

Technologies are ways of influencing resources in the production process. New man-made technologies expand the possibilities of using the properties of resources and allow the development of waste-free or low-waste environmentally friendly technologies. Eternal development technologies include all the means and resources to ensure eternal life.

Technology management in the direction of eternal development can be done through the number series **9187114 319 19**

Energy is the driving force that transforms natural resources in order to create wealth. The energy necessary for the eternal life of each person is in the area of harmonious interaction between people and the environment aimed at achieving eternal development. The method of obtaining energy sufficient for the eternal development of all is expressed by the following number series: **918 09814.** This number series can be mentally repeated «sub vocally» several times a day during any activity and obtained with its use rejuvenation.

The information factor is the search, collection, processing, storage and dissemination of useful information necessary for human production activities. In the system of eternal development, he often forms the effectiveness of the methods of eternal development. The role of this factor in modern conditions has grown dramatically and has an impact on the entire market economy, predetermining the choice of consumers and producers at the microeconomic level.

The number series **964 819 3189891** can be used to form the information factor of eternal development. This series with the addition of three numbers **914** in front of it can be used in the processes of resurrection when doing business. The resurrection of people for a successful business is important, as it allows not to lose specialists and just workers who are able to work in the chosen business area. Therefore, in business areas, the approach to resurrection issues should be pragmatic and business-like, based on the goal of making a profit. The introduction of the task of resurrecting people in business technology can be done by special orientation of the information factor related to this.

Ecology is the interaction of man with the environment. Any production activity of a person directly or indirectly related to the impact on the environment. For eternal development, ecology development must correspond to the task being performed. The number series for eternal ecological development: **31914 51678109849**

The result of the interaction of factors of production is the creation of benefits, the direction of which for eternal development is determined by the number series: **913 518 906318**

The numbers corresponding to the terms are used to ensure eternal development with the help of the concepts and processes described by these terms. The result of the interaction of factors of production is the creation of benefits, the direction of which for eternal development is determined by the number series: **913 518 906318**

The numbers corresponding to the terms are used to ensure eternal development with the help of the concepts and processes described by these terms.

NUMBER SERIES IN ALPHABETIC ORDER

A

ABSOLUTE ECONOMIC EFFICIENCY (TOTAL) 316518498917 – Effectiveness of capital investments' implementations in the national economy, in economic region, in industry, in construction of new and also reconstruction of existing enterprises, etc.

ACCELERATED DEPRECIATION 719 649518 714 – is a method that allows you to transfer most of the cost of fixed assets to finished products in the first years of their operation.

ACCEPTANCE 51831849561471 – consent to conclude an agreement under certain conditions; form of non-cash payments.

ACCOUNTING 716518319478 – is a system of constant accounting and control over the use of funds and inventory.

ACCOUNTING BALANCE 481617319514 – is an integral part of accounting.

ACCOUNTING RATE OF INCOME 314513318451 – the share of average net profit received from the implementation of the investment project and attributable to the amount of advance cash capital (cost of the investment project).

ACCOUNTS PAYABLE 564812319481 – Temporary taken by an institution monetary means which are due to be returned to creditor including payment of appropriate interests for given loan.

ACCOUNTS RECEIVAVBLE 314828 498717 – is the result of economic activity when the enterprise collects the amount of debts due to it.

ACT 984 316 519880168 – A document drawn up by a commission of several persons and confirms established facts or events.

ACTIVE 319819497817 - is the left side of the balance sheet, which reflects the property rights of the enterprise and includes fixed assets, normalized and irregular working capital and other assets.

ACTIVE CAPITAL PRODUCTIVITY 319317219498 – Assets ratio, which is based not on the total value of fixed assets, but only on the value of their active part.

ACTIVE PART OF THE MAIN PRODUCTION FUNDS 519317498516481 - is an integral and leading part of the main production assets, which serves as a basis for assessing the technical level of production capacities.

ACTUAL WAGE 614814219617 – Numerical estimate of opportunity of material benefits and services getting (purchasing) on a nominal wage.

ACTUAL OPERATING TIME OF THE EQUIPMENT UNIT 501 648719491 - is the time required to produce a certain volume of production.

ADDED VALUE 19156481918 - is a part of the new value that is created by workers with the help of surplus time and fully assigned by the manufacturer.

ADMINISTRATIVE AND COMMAND ECONOMY 519648319 817 - is an economic system based on the concentration in the hands of the state of all developed and approved economic directives in the field of production, distribution and exchange of material goods.

ADDITIONAL DISTRIBUTION COST 614 812719 418 - Expenditures arisen when in use in the course of production process (transportation, storage, and so on) in the sphere of turnover.

ADDITIONAL PROFIT 519 618516 714 - is typical for capital export. It expresses an exceeding profit for advanced monetary capital in comparison with its return inside the country.

ADDITIONAL SALARY 689 718514371 - payments provided for by law and labor agreement, for example, payment of regular and additional vacations.

ADVANCE 398628198711 - Monetary means or property values are construed as funds of enterprise provided with fixed in the contract accomplishment of mandatory conditions.

ADVANCED MANUFACTURING 64121489871 - New construction, extension and conversion of existing plants and other industrial facilities, carried on with the approved project cost estimates.

ADVANCE 914719318 916 - advance payment of the amount of money against wages or part of the contractual price for the development of the project, order, etc.

ADVERTISING 518617319478 - measures for wide dissemination of information about the company's goods and services, reflecting technical and economic characteristics and advantages over analogues and substitutes.

AFTER-SALES SERVICE 498 217219 81 - free services provided to the consumer during the warranty period after payment for the goods.

AFTER-MARKET DEMAND 317 694 318 817 - demand for the product, which is in direct proportion to the demand for other goods.

ALLOWANCE FOR PRICES 614217519498 – system for additional premium to a price acted as a deterrence for rate of transformation of cheap goods into deficit ones.

ALLOCATIVE EFFICIENCY 561418519471 - the most rational distribution of organic resources towards their final use.

ALTERNATIVE EXPENDITURES 489 712319 614 – current cost of production which is directly dependent from production volume for instance basic materials, salary of production and related workers and so on.

ANALYSIS OF EXISTING MARKETS BY OBJECTS 514819319617 - provides for the relevant types of work on the following objects of study: sphere of commodity circulation - purchase and sale procedure to ensure profit; product of labor created for exchange and sale; legal or individuals who consume industrial products; competition.

ANALYSIS OF THE ECONOMIC ACTIVITY OF THE ENTERPRISE 589614219712 - is a method of a comprehensive study of the results of the activities of an industrial enterprise and its divisions.

ANALYSIS OF THE ECONOMIC ACTIVITY OF THE ENTERPRISE - COMPETITOR 598317984314 - the direction of scientific research of current and strategic plans for the development of the rival enterprise.

ANNUAL ECONOMIC EFFECT 519 618219 717 – is the result of economic activity, which is calculated by the compared variants of capital investment embodiments. It is the difference between the reduced costs, adjusted for annual production volume.

ANTI-COMPETITIVE PRACTICE 491318516497 - organizational work on planning and implementation of measures to reduce and completely eliminate recurrent problems related to competition in the market.

ANTI-MONOPOLY POLICY OF THE STATE 59831849714 – state policy directed to competition development and creation of limits for monopoly activity of participants working under condition of market competition.

APPEAL FUND 548319619718 - is a fund that ensures the continuity of the production and sale of the company's products.

APPLIED INDUSTRY RESEARCH AND DEVELOPMENT 49871431981 - new technical solutions with tasks and proposals aimed at to improve the competitiveness of production and production.

ARTICLE QUALITY PER STANDARD 718421619417 - Quality of goods (and services) which meets technical specifications or standards corresponding to requirements of bilateral agreement between manufacturer and consumer.

ASSECURATION 54831489518 – Insurance of finished products, movable and immovable property.

ASSESSMENT BASIS 718481061498 - Aggregation of income of physical persons or corporate bodies subjected to taxation.

ASSESSMENT OF BASIC PRODUCTION ASSETS 614813519714 – Methods used to estimate the recoverable amount, i.e., of the value, which reflects the time necessary for the reproduction of the goods at present.

ASSESSMENT OF COMPETITIVENESS 489718 - Evaluation of the financial position and capacity of the borrower to repay the loan.

ASSESSMENT OF WORK PLACES 518648798181 – Estimation of working places on the basis of integrity of technical, economical and managerial factors for developing of organizing and technical arrangements' plan for provision of consistency in labor conditions and change of non-efficient operations of working process when necessary.

ASSETS 516 719418 - material, funds, property used for settlements of payments and repayment of debts on obligations.

ASSET 319819497817 «Left side of the balance sheet» – which reflects the economic rights of the enterprise and includes fixed assets, normalized and non-normalized working capital and other assets.

ASSORTMENT 49131851847 - products of the same name, grouped by certain criteria: quality, brand, size, type, etc.

ATTRACTED FUNDS 59861731849 - borrowed funds in the form of state or commercial loans to replenish working capital.

AUDIT 69831459878 - verification of the financial and economic activities of legal entities in order to objectively assess the performance of the functions established by law.

AUDIT CHAMBER 217214219317 - governmental organization which has control over the generation, distribution and use of public funds.

AUDIT SERVICE 514318519417 - individuals or legal entities with permission from state bodies to perform the function of checking the state of financial and economic activities of the organization.

AUCTION 598491319814 - is a type of sale of goods (property) on the basis of preliminary inspection of the auction objects put up for sale.

AUDITING SERVICE 514318519417 – Corporate bodies or individuals possessed a license for performing of financial economic enterprise of an enterprise's activity, check functions.

AUDITOR 319471897185 - organization, service, auditor-accountant, auditing the financial and economic activities of enterprises, banks, etc.

AUTHORIZED CAPITAL 649 748219 817 - Source of formation of fixed assets and working capital of the enterprise with the use of budgetary allocations, funds of founders and members and shares contributions.

AUTHORIZED CAPITAL «Joint Stock» 564217894274 – Aggregated means' cost stipulated by article of association or a joint-venture agreement (Joint Stock Company).

AUTOMATED DATA BANK 519617 – Systematic information (program, methodological, technical, philological, economic, etc.) accumulated and used to ensure timely satisfaction of the needs and interests in various forms of activity.

AUTOMATION 519319718 49 - application of machines, machinery and technologies in order to carry out production, management and other functions under the direct control of a person.

AVERAGE AGE OF EQUIPMENT 819498796315 - is the average age of the equipment park.

AVERAGE ANNUAL COST OF MAIN PRODUCTION FUNDS 798 694219 917 - is an indicator reflecting the change in value during the year as a result of new and disposal of physically worn and morally established fixed assets.

AVERAGE ANNUAL COST OF PRODUCTION FUNDS 594 712319 614 - the sum of the average annual value of the main production assets and working capital.

AVERAGE ANNUAL NUMBER OF EMPLOYEES 519 618319491 - quantitative assessment of the list personnel of the enterprise on average for a certain period (month, quarter, year).

AVERAGE ANNUAL VALUE OF WORKING CAPITAL 564 813319 814 - calculated as the average chronological, the input and disposal of working capital are timed to the middle of the month.

AXCISE 518716319419819 - Type of indirect taxes which are is an integral part of release price and is to be charged to budget completely. It has to be set for consumer goods generally.

B

BACKLOG«ACCUMULATION» 368214289716 - Product which has not passed the whole cycle of technological operations.

BALANCE 519 714819 718 - the difference between cash receipts (debit) and expenses (credit) of the enterprise, firm for a certain period (month, quarter, year).

BALANCE BETWEEN SUPLY AND DEMAND 471819514317 -One of conditions of market economy adjustment which reflects consistence of manufacturing product volume with demand structure.

BALANCE OF INCOME AND EXPENSES 71948919814 - is the financial result of the enterprise, assessed in monetary form on the basis of a system of technical and economic indicators.

BALANCE SHEET 481617319514 - Integral part of accounting.

BALANCE VALUE 51489119489 - the initial cost of fixed assets (main capital), which includes the cost of purchasing tools (for buildings and structures - the estimated cost of construction), taking into account their transportation and installation.

BALANCED BUDGET 317814898517 – income and expenses estimate that has zero balance in money terms.

BALANCE SHEET VALUE 548 614891 498 - the value of fixed assets and intangible assets at which they are used for accounting.

BANKRUPTCY 316548319714 - recognized by the authorities lack the payment ability of the debtor to satisfy in full the claims of creditors on monetary obligations or to fulfill the obligation to make mandatory government payments.

BANCRUPTCY «insolvency» 58941418517 – insolvency, inability of corporate body or physical person to pay for bond of obligation due to absence of cash means.

BANK 318614564817 – is a credit and financial organization whose important functions are to accumulate temporarily free funds and provide them on credit to other organizations.

BANK CAPITAL 31482121847- is a set of delicate capital, both own and attracted, operated by the bank to protect fixed assets from premature physical wear and tear.

BANK LOAN 31848561947 - the amount of funds provided to individuals and legal entities for a certain period of time at the established interest rate.

BANK NOTE 314816719481 - variety of cash means issued for making loan operations on security of goods, promissory note, soft money (bank notes) emission of which is predetermined with circulation and outgoing.

BANK TICKET 314816719481 - is a type of money issued for loan operations secured by goods, promissory notes; paper money (banknotes), the issue of which is predetermined by circulation and payments.

BANK TRANSFER 94821729878 – calculations carried out without the involvement of money by transferring of amounts from current or checking account of the payer (buyer) to the beneficiary (seller).

BANKING CAPITAL 31482121847 – Aggregate of monetary capitals either owned or raised with which bank is operating.

BARTER DEAL 487198598641 - direct cashless exchange. The main reason for barter transactions is currency and monetary problems.

BASE 318471819712 - economic indicators used as a basis for comparison with other indicators.

BASE YEAR 581318718492 - is a year taken as a basis for calculating the rate of change in indicators and indices.

BASIC PRODUCTION ASSETS' RETIREMENT RATE 514 491619 71 - Indicator defined as the ratio of the value of the basic production assets liquidated, written off the balance sheet of the enterprise to their value at the beginning of the year.

BASIC RESEARCH 514212819471 - line of research devoted to the study of the objective natural laws, laws of society, the productive forces and the scientific basis for the design of new equipment, technology, etc.

BASIS TERMS OF DELIVERY 514031489604 - special conditions of purchase and sale, which are issued in the form of an invitation (contract).

BILATERAL MONOPOLY 39867121878 - Market circumstances presented with one seller and one buyer.

BILATERAL OLIGOPOLY 89751421961 - Market circumstances expressing by high concentration of sellers and buyers.

BILL OF ACCEPTANCE 51831849561471 - Acceptance of concluding agreement under certain conditions; cashless settlement form.

BOND CARGO 489 716519481 - - imported goods stored in a customs warehouse with subsequent payment of customs duty.

BOND OF OBLIGATION 314812219417 - Executed in written obligation of corporate body or individual confirming the timeliness of taken from creditor loan return. Loan may be non-interest-bearing and subject to payment of interests for credit.

BOOK VALUE 51489119489 - Initial price of fixed production assets (capital asset), which included price of instruments of labor purchasing (for buildings, premises -construction budget) including transportation and mounting.

BORROW FUNDS 548 491319614 - source of circulating capital, the funds received in the form of bank loans (credit) and from other sources which is temporarily held by the Company and are used along with its own working capital.

BORROWER 314821318491 - is an individual or legal entity that undertakes, in accordance with the concluded agreement, to return the loan received from the creditor within the prescribed period and pay the appropriate interest for the used loan.

BORROWED FUNDS 548 491319614 - source of working capital formation; funds received in the form of a bank loan (credit) and other sources, temporarily at the disposal of the enterprise and used on an equal basis with its own working capital.

BORROWED FUNDS «short-term» 314964818571 - is part of working capital, the source of which is a short-term loan.

BORROWED LOANS 59861731849 – borrowed funds in the form of governmental or commercial loans for working capital replenishment.

BORROWER 314821318491 – Individual or corporate body which is liable according to concluded contract to return in due time received from creditor borrowing and to pay appropriate interests for used credit.

"BOTTLENECK" 431 489516 71 – a situation resulting from shortcomings in the organization of production, when the working place is not provided with material, labor or fuel and energy resources; excess of labor productivity during the previous technological operation (or equipment capacity) over labor productivity during subsequent operation, arising after the lack of congruence of the main technological equipment park.

BRAINS DRAIN 315 478498 671 – is the process of intellectual workers leaving their country of and highly qualified workers for permanent residence (or time) in another country.

BREAK-EVEN « covered by income (revenue)**» 498 712819 49** – principle of high enterprise or firm performance according to which all expenses incurred for the simple reproduction should be covered by income (revenue) from the sale of manufactured products.

BREAK-EVEN 714819319471 – the volume of sales of goods, the proceeds from the sale of which are identical to the cost of production.

BREAK-EVEN CURVE 614812519471 – is a curve that graphically illustrates the condition under which the current production costs are equal to the proceeds from the sale of manufactured products.

BREAK-EVEN POINT 483 488519 471 – is the level of production of products at which the proceeds from its sale is equal to the current costs of its production.

BROKER 518471219516 – is an intermediary that carries out transactions for the purchase and sale of goods and securities on exchanges on exchanges on behalf of interested parties (buyer and seller) and at their expense.

BUDGET 564318517318 – is a balanced estimate of income and expenses, compiled in monetary terms for a certain period.

BUDGET BALANCED 317814898517 - an estimate of income and expenses in monetary terms, which has a zero balance.

BUDGET FOR THE PREPARATION AND DEVELOPMENT OF PRODUCTION 548 671319 894 – Estimate, which is made by newly developed products or technologies for each unit of the enterprise, and then reduced to a single estimate with a deciphering of expenses for the calculation items and cost components.

BUDGET SURPLUS 618317914912 – excess of income over expenditure.

BUSINESS 194198514716 – economic activity carried out at the expense of own or borrowed funds at its own risk and under its own responsibility in order to generate income, were.

BUSINESS GAME 518618994817 – modeling of real operating conditions of the enterprise, company in order to identify production reserves and eliminate deviations of the main technical and economic indicators from the planned ones.

BUSINESS INDEPENDENT 71974131981 – independent activity of individuals or legal entities, aimed at generating of income, the maximum profit from the sale of goods, works and services.

BUSINESS CYCLE 619314 801316846 – cycle stages, i.e., peak, recession, crisis, depression, recovery, rise.

BUSINESS PLAN 486148519819 – is the main program of entrepreneurial activities of the company, including economically sound organizational and technical measures.

BUYER'S DEBT 316318819412 - is an unpaid share of the value of goods sold on credit.

BUYER'S DEBT COEFFICIENT 314 712819 71 - the share of the value of goods sold in a child in the total value of the goods to be sold.

BUYER MARKET 81971298749 - is an economic situation in the market in which prices decrease as a result of over-accommodation, i.e. the value of supply at current prices exceeds the value of demand.

BUYER PRICE 691 718219 71 - is the upper limit of the price that the consumer of goods (services) can pay.

BUYING POWER 714 718194 71 - the ability to purchase goods (services) per monetary unit.

BY-PRODUCT 519 614 –is a product (goods) that is created simultaneously in the process of manufacturing the main product.

CALCULATION ACCOUNT 319718904614 - is a document reflecting the availability of free funds temporarily stored in credit and financial institutions. It is used in cash settlements with individuals and legal entities.

ACCOUNTS CHAMBER 217214219317 - is a government organization that controls the formation, distribution and use of public funds.

CALCULATION OF PRIME COST 498312319714 - Calculation of current cost of production per unit of product according to cost items.

CALENDAR TIME FUND 584319489417 - The maximum operating time of the equipment during the year.

CAPACITY 4817190 478 - legal possibilities of businesses and individuals to create and protect the property and personal rights and responsibilities.

CAPACITY UTILIZATION 568318498217 - Level of used available production potentials which are to be estimated with ratio of actual product output to maximum possible output.

CAPITAL 69831421947 - is an economic category that reflects the value of means of production, which, when using labor, create added value. Capital is subdivided into fixed assets (fixed assets) and working capital (current funds) and can act as monetary, industrial and statutory.

CAPITAL «of private property» 514 719 – Part of productive capital, the characteristic for conditions of private property.

CAPITAL ACCUMULATION 6194831947 – materialization of part of the profit in fixed assets for the development or technical re-equipment of the enterprise.

CAPITAL LABOR RATIO 31961421971 – Average annual value of fixed assets attributed to one of average employees.

CAPITAL INVESTMENTS 69891421947 – Actual investments, nonrecurrent expenditures for prime extended reproduction of basic production assets, i.e., for new building, extension, reconstruction and technical re-equipment of operating enterprises and also erecting, repair and technique implementation of facilities intended for non-production functions.

CAPITAL IVESTMENTS ECONOMIC EFFICIENCY 518317219491 – Indicator of feasibility of the one-time expenditures making, based on the comparison of the resulting effect «savings, income, etc. And capital investments which ensure the result.

CAPITAL FLIGHT - 48131951847 – export of real money or currency from the state to other countries in order to avoid losses from possible economic or political crises.

CAPITAL MOVEMENT 388519397544 – Relocation of means from one enterprise to another enterprise within the limits of one industry, from one industry to another industry either within limits of one country or between countries for the purposes of higher profit attainment per invested capital unit.

CAPITAL INTENCITY OF PRODUCTS OR SERVICES UNIT

514 718517 485 – an indicator of the cost of fixed assets per unit product or service.

CAPITAL PRODUCTIVITY 317518614217 – synthesis rate, characterizing the use of fixed assets.

CAPITAL RETURN ON INVESTMENT 489 714819 714 - is an indicator reflecting the period during which advance capital investments are affected by savings or profits derived from the materialization of capital investments.

CAPITAL TURNOVER TIME 518491 617914 - is the period during which the industrial capital advanced for the production of surplus value goes through all stages of turnover (commodity, productive, monetary). A year is taken as a unit of measurement and comparison of the time of turnover.

CAPITALIZATION 698581319471 – Estimation method for enterprise cost according to income received from the use of property over a certain period.

CAPITALIZATION UNIT 648518798417 - the cost of an element of fixed assets (machines, equipment, building, construction, etc.), fixed in the capital cost account.

CAPITAL PRODUCTIVITY RATIO 31861731849 - Share of national income increment related to one monetary unit of capital investment.

CAPITALIZATION RATIO INCREMENTAL 319718219614 – capital ratio of incremental index, which is used in assessing the impact of various factors on the use level of fixed assets over the study period.

CARTEL 498718648481 - Variety of monopoly integration of large-scale goods manufacturers of similar product for the purposes of competitive activity weakening and increase of sales volume on the basis of agreement on re-distribution of sphere of influence in the product markets, i.e., on the basis of stated certain share of sales at the agreed price for each participant of agreement.

CASH FLOW 318612518714 - funds entering the current account of the enterprise from the sale of products and the provision of services, as well as from other sources. It is used to cover current costs and other purposes.

CASHLESS SETTLEMENTS 94821729878 - settlements made without the participation of funds by transferring amounts from the current or current account of the payer (buyer) to the account of the recipient (seller).

CENTRALIZATION OF CAPITAL 721 482819 617 - merger of small producers and financial organizations into larger business unions and financial prices.

CERTIFICATE 514 218719 61 - certificate confirming the compliance of the product with technical specifications or certain standards for a certain period.

CERTIFICATION OF WORKPLACES 518648798181 - assessment of workplaces based on a set of technical, economic and organizational indicators to develop a plan of organizational and technical measures to ensure their compliance with modern requirements for working conditions and in case of the need to replace inefficient operations of the labor process.

CHAMBER OF COMMERCE AND INDUSTRY 485 471898 17 - is a Governmental organization that acts as a legal entity to promote the development of economic, scientific, technical and trade relations.

CHANNELS OF DISTRIBUTION OF GOODS 61949831947 - the sequence of promotion of goods from the manufacturer to the buyer.

CHIFT INDEX 589 842819 64 – An indicator of assessment of the equipment operation time uses per a shift on the whole, which is calculated as a ratio of the number of products of working days by machines number during a working day to the total number of installed equipment.

CHOICE OF TARGET MARKET SEGMENTS 564197589491 – Estimate and choice of one or several segments of market for entry into with own goods.

CIRCULAR 319 317498641 - a letter informing other company or person concerned on the planned event or a fait accompli.

CIRCULATION FUND 548319619718 - fund, which ensures continuity of the process of the company production and sales.

CLASSIFICATION 489482719481 - Ranking of subjects, entities and notions into groups, classes on the basis of similarity of such and such classification characteristics.

CLEAN COMPETITION MARKET 71849851971 - is a market situation where there are a large number of producers and consumers who manufacture and buy similar specialized goods.

CLEAN MONOPOLY MARKET 51948921964 - is a type of competition in which the sale of goods on the market is organized by a single manufacturer, while there is no competition and there are various benefits and privileges from the state.

CLEARING 519471219641 – System of mutual cashless settlements for purchasing-sales of goods and material values and rendering of services.

CLOSE CORPORATION (CC) 21498751949 - Company, stocks of which are to be distributed among its participants or according to the list confirmed beforehand.

CLOSEDOWN OF BUSINESS 519 618719 216 – Temporary break of industrial enterprise activity for the purpose of fulfillment of technical measures intended to prevent key assets from early physical depreciation.

COEFFICIENT FOR USAGE OF WORKING AREA 619 717 218 918 – Ratio defined as the ratio of the gross or commercial products cost in a given period (day, month and year) to the total production area, i.e., it is the cost of production attributed to $1m^2$ of production area.

COEFFICIENT OF BASE EQUIPMENT CONTINGENCY 491819317481 – An indicator reflecting the ratio of the interaction of possibilities of each interchangeable equipment group included in the production chain of processing of parts included in the finished product.

COEFFICIENT OF COHESION OF THE MAIN TECHNOLOGICAL EQUIPMENT PARK 491819317481 - is an indicator reflecting the ratio of the capabilities of each group of interchangeable equipment included in the technological chain of processing parts included in the finished product.

COEFFICIENT OF DEMENSIONAL PARAMETERS USAGE 514 617518 719 - Indicator of the intensity of equipment use, defined as the ratio in which the numerator is a sum each term of which is the product of one-dimensional interval of a part by load factor of machine with parts of the interval, and the denominator in the product of one of the dimensional parameters of the machine by a factor of the machine utilization.

COEFFICIENT OF PHYSICAL DETERIORATION OF THE EQUIPMENT 53012450818 - An indicator presented the share of the original cost of the equipment carried forward the finished product.

COEFFICIENT OF ELASTICY 518 619419 714 – Percentage change in the quantity of goods sold per one percent change in the price of goods (products).

COEFFICIENT OF USE OF PRODUCTION AREAS 619 717218 918 - coefficient defined as the ratio of the value of gross or commercial products. For a certain period (day, month, year) to the total production area, i.e., it is the cost of production per 1 meter squared of production area.

COEFFICIENT OF USE OF REPLACEABLE RE-PRESSURE OF EQUIPMENT 421 478561 471 - ratio of the actual shift coefficient to the mode of operation of the equipment.

COLLECTION OF PAYMENTS 819419419718 - Type of mediatory bank operation, exercised according to the client order for accept and placing to a transaction account of the principal of the monetary means from enterprises and institutions purchased from principal the material and goods values, including payment for accomplishment (rendering) of services.

COLLECTION RATIO 314 712819 71 - The share of cost of goods sold on credit to the total value of the goods that are due to sell.

COLLECTIVE AGREEMENT 564812219718 - Mutual agreement which is concluded between labor team and administration representatives of an enterprise on mutual responsibilities and conditions of reconciling of disputes in the course of production and business activity.

COMBINE 49164 321 819061 - Amalgamation of several technologically connected to each other enterprises of various industry sector.

COMBINING 49831721948 - Form of industrial production concentration which stipulated amalgamation in one enterprise (complex) of the several specific and mutually connected enterprises of different branches consequently performed technological operations for processing of raw materials i.e., product of one manufacturing is to be material for another manufacturing process.

COMMISSIONING OF THE MAIN PRODUCTION FUNDS 564181798164 - planned commissioning of new, reconstructed and expanded capital construction facilities.

COMMAND ECONOMY 519648319 817 - An economic system based on the concentration in the hands of the state of all developed and approved economic guidelines for the production, distribution and exchange of wealth.

COMMERCIAL AGREEMENT 498 617319714 - Agreement between corporate bodies (enterprises, firms) in which standards, regulations and liabilities of production and sales of goods, rendering of services are notified.

COMMERCIAL BANK 648317319718 - Non-governmental credit institution which is working on the commercial basis, dedicated to giving monetary loans to corporate bodies on mutually beneficial principles and to rendering of services for private clients on commission basis.

COMMERCIAL CREDIT 564812719478 - Loan presented in commodity terms at the moment of fulfillment of deal i.e., with delay of payment for purchasing or delivered goods.

COMMERCIAL ENTERPRISE 519316418218 - Corporate body working under conditions of self-financing and aimed at profit earning. Commercial enterprise is acting generally in the sphere of goods and services circulation.

COMMERCIALIZATION 574891719516 - One of the privatization stages when all responsibility for enterprise activity results is bearing by administration, the state at that stops to assign subsidy for loss reimbursement.

COMMISSION 519621798317 - Bilateral agreement on the basis of which one party (commissioner) is obliged to exercise deals on behalf of another party (consignor) as instructed by consignor.

COMMISSION AGENT 319612719814 – Intermediary who exercises procedure of purchasing-sale of goods for established remuneration as instructed by a guarantee.

COMMODITY CONJUNCTURE 319 688316 491 - the position of a certain product in the market, characterized by the ratio of supply and demand of this product and the dynamics of its change under the influence of various factors.

COMMODITY AND MATERIAL VALUES 518 671219 49 - is an integral part of working capital that provides uninterrupted production and economic activities of the enterprise and includes the cost of production stocks, remains of work in progress and finished products.

COMMODITY HEADING 719 617219 818 - Competitiveness of goods, which is partially or fully complies with the requirements of consumers and has a definite position in the market.

COMMODITY ITEM 719 617219 818 - is the level of competitiveness of goods that partially or fully meets the requirements of consumers and occupies a certain position in the commodity market.

COMMODITY PRODUCER 497 214318 471 - Natural person or legal entity that organizes the production.

COMMODITY STOCKS 518 671294 498 - Finished products prepared for sale and located in the sphere of circulation of commodities, that is, in the warehouse, in transit etc.

COMPANY 219948938471 - Enterprise purposes to organize commercial or industrial activity.

COMPANY 47131421981 - Industrial, commercial or economic enterprise, endowed with legal entity rights.

COMPANY'S ENERGY RESOURCES 61931851964 – Aggregate of all types of energy, and energy carriers (power machines, transformer devices, and other energy sources used in the production and distribution of energy in the company), providing of the manufacturing process and other energy needs (lighting, heating, etc.).

COMPARATIVE ADVANTAGES 516 319318 617 - a set of features that allow you to choose the most economical version of the event, resource, money, etc.

COMPARABLE PRODUCTS 57484851418 – is a set of products manufactured in the planning period, the mass and serial development of which dates back to the previous year.

COMPARABILITY OF CAPITAL INVESTMENT EFFICIENCY OPTIONS 698 798719418 - is a method used in the implementation of scientific and technological progress when there are several options for economic solutions Time and current costs, but also production volumes.

COMPETITION IN PRODUCT MARKETS 719 612794 489 - Division of business plan for which there are classified results of analysis of conditions of production and sales for principal competitors according to factors' listing of competitive capability: goods (quality, technical and economic indicators and etc.), price (sales, credit conditions and etc.), sales channels, sales volumes' growth achievement (advertisement, participation in tenders and biddings, fairies and etc.)

COMPETITIVE ABILITIES 8906 14 489159 8417 – Integrity of technical and economic characteristics of goods advantageously differed from analogous article at extent of satisfying of consumer interests of buyer.

COMPETITIVE ABILITY OF PRODUCTION 589612 619417 – Evaluation of technical and economic opportunities for achievement of manufacturer and consumer interests' concordance.

COMPETITIVENESS ASSESSMENT 489718 - assessment of the financial situation and capabilities of the borrower to repay the loan in a timely manner.

COMPETITIVE STRATEGY 698317594181 - Aggregation of economic measures targeted at sales growth provision at established price of supplied for the market goods.

COMPLAINT 58421871947 - an official statement containing a claim for unsatisfactory fulfillment of the requirements of the buyer (customer) in relation to the purchased goods (performance of services).

COMPLEX 49164 321 819061 - Amalgamation of several technologically connected to each other enterprises of different industry sectors.

COMPOUND INTEREST 498 728519 742 - Factor, which is used to determine the amount of the credit and determine the base for the calculation of payments on investments.

CONCERN 568 714918 214 - Large-scale amalgamation of corporate bodies of industrial, financial or trade sectors for the purposes of single management ascertainment along with limited business independence of enterprises and firms included.

CONDITIONS OF CONTRACT 794 718319 671 - Legally agreed bilateral or multilateral treaty, in which there are recorded: the conditions of sale, description of goods, the price, the terms of obligations, as well as the mutual rights and obligations of the parties.

CONDITIONAL PRODUCTS 619 728518 641 - newly created value, which is the difference between the cost of marketable products (in wholesale prices of the enterprise) and material costs (salary, profit, amortization).

CONDITIONAL SAVINGS 548 691319 814 – estimated value - on savings as a result of the introduction of scientific and technological progress into the production process or the implementation of other organizational measures included in the plan.

CONFIDENCE LEVEL 678 491316 497 – **Technical-economical assessment for** the influence of each parameter included in the corresponding group of technical and economic parameters that determine the relative level of competitiveness of production or products.

CONFLICT 589617 498 71 – Incompatibility, inconsistency of interests in socio-labor relations; disagreement between concerned parties.

CONJUNCTURE 318 682798 214 – External and internal circumstances (factors) immediately influenced on production process and monetary means circulation.

CONJUNCTURE OF MARKET 594 712489 216 – Trade circumstances depended on a correlation of demand and supply values, price flexibility and other socio-economic and natural factors at goods market during appropriate period.

CONSORTIUM 219 214819717 – is a temporary contract for the production and marketing cooperation of several industrial organizations for the joint implementation of a large industrial project.

CONSTANT EXPENDITURES (DISPROPORTIONATE) 498316319712 – Expenses (expenditures for heating, illumination, total factory and shop floors expenditures and so on) which do not vary substantially when production volume is changing.

CONSTRUCTION BUDGET 519 648518 742 – Cost necessary for the construction and commissioning of fixed assets in accordance with the approved project.

CONSULTING 56482131947 – Rendering of services for market economy entities' (buyers, vendors, product manufacturers) consulting towards questions of organizing, enterprises and firm's economy management and etc.

CONSULTING COMPANY 549491819471 - are special organizations that advise industrial enterprises and individual individuals on current problems of economics, law and finance.

CONSUMER 216498517 – is a physical or legal person who meets his need as a result of the purchase of goods (services).

CONSUMER AND RETAIL PRICE INDEX 319618519412 - is a monthly published indicator that characterizes changes (dynamics) in the cost of a set of goods and services necessary to meet the priority needs of the population in the area (consumer basket) and the average level of prices in the retail market.

CONSUMER LOAN 548 671319 71 - deferred payment for goods.

CONSUMER PROPERTIES OF GOODS 819517214718 - a set of aesthetic and technical and production properties of the labor product that ensure the most complete satisfaction of the buyer's needs.

CONSUMER PRICE 518 491319 614 - the ability of goods (services) to meet certain needs of the population and material production.

CONSUMER ITEMS 47517489481 – part of the social product provided to meet individual and collective needs.

CUSTOMER ARREARS 316318819412 – unpaid cost share of goods sold on credit

CONSUMPTION ITEMS 47517489481 - is an integral part of a social product designed to meet personal and collective needs.

CONSUMPTION 648517 – the use of material goods or services to satisfy the personal or industrial interest of an individual or legal entity.

CONTRACT 498514 618 498 – is a legal bilateral or multilateral contract that fixes the rights and obligations of each party.

CONTRACT 519 716 718 498514 – Agreement of purchase and sale between purchaser and seller on conditions of receipt of money on credit (loan, borrowing and so on), changes of rights and liabilities of parties.

CONTRACT OF DELIVERY 574 814319 614 – Agreement to be concluded between production enterprises on delivery of goods by enterprise manufacturer of material values (raw materials, stuff, components, finished product and so on) to enterprise – consumer with notification of terms and volume of delivery, goods quality, price, package payment and so on.

CONTRACT OF THE SALE OF GOODS 516 718498 712 – Condition of handover by seller of rights to consumer on the basis of concluded agreement in which mutual liabilities, conditions of delivery and acceptance of goods taking into account its features, established standards and quality requirements are expressing.

CONTRACT TERMS 794 718319 671 - legally agreed bilateral or multilateral contract, where the following are specified: terms of sale, characteristics of the goods, price, term of performance of obligations, as well as mutual rights and obligations of the parties.

CONTRACTUAL PRICE 8 491 697 818 - price established on the basis of an agreement between the manufacturer (seller) and the consumer (buyer).

CONTRIBUTIONS TO THE BUDGET 319 714 - payments to the budget, which are made by enterprises, firms: income tax, value added tax, excise taxes, property tax.

CONTROL AS A FUNTION OF ENTERPRICE MANAGEMENT 648 218548 714 – assessment of compliance of the results of the enterprise's work with the requirements of the instructions for the implementation of qualitative and quantitative indicators of economic and social development.

CONTROL DEVICES AND APPLIANCE 548697498 – part of fixed assets.

CONTROL FIGURES 564 891 498718 - non-directive information reflecting the quantitative and qualitative conditions necessary for planning socio-economic development.

CONTROL STOCK 694 817918514 – Share of stocks allowed owner (individual or corporate body) to perform full management over joint stock company activity. Control stock has to exceed 50% of principal value of issued by joint stock company shares, in any separate cases 25–30% will be enough.

CONTROLLING 619 217218 497 – coordination management and information support of the process of achieving the final goals of the enterprise on the basis of generalization of accounting, analysis, planned and control results of economic activity.

CONVERSION 698518548491 – Output product structure change; conversion of defense industry enterprises into production of civilian goods.

CONVERSION MARKETING 564813319481 – Absence of buyers' interest for purchasing goods or services. For instance, diabetics do not buy sugar, confectionary and etc.

COOPERATIVE 895 718495 164 – Model of voluntary amalgamation for participation in manufacturing or consumer business on the basis of mutual collective (share) property.

COPYRIGHT 519 418 712 – the right of a legal entity or individual to publish and sell the results of creative and intellectual work.

CORPORATE BODY 518 612319 718 – organization, company, firm, which in accordance with the law appears to be an independent bearer of rights and duties and have the main characteristics of the legal entity.

CORPORATE STOCK 61489231857 - a cash contribution of an individual or legal entity that allows you to acquire certain rights to own the property of a joint-stock company, etc.

CORPORATIVISM 561 491598 64 – thrust of institutional transformation based on union or conjunction of industrial enterprises and financial institutions (industrial and financial groups) in business interests socializing for creation of economic advantages at the expense of monetary and industrial capital concentration taking into account a labor.

CORRUPTION 584 721591 68 – criminal offence based on a duty holder's (including political and public personalities) use of rights conferred for actions punishable by law (one-time or constant functional orders) that paid for by means of bribes.

COST 218498 461 - labor embodied in the product; purpose for goods or services.

COST ADDED 648517219 648 - the cost of goods minus the cost of materials spent on the production of this product.

COST 51421961871 - The cost of purchasing tools (price), including the cost of transportation and installation, and for capital construction estimated cost.

COST CALCULATION 498312319714 - calculation of current production costs per unit of production by cost.

COST CONTROL 498 471213 485 - Governmental cumulative measures for regulation of retail and wholesale prices by the way of acceptance of limited factors for the growth.

COST INCREASE 61931981947 - a set of costs incurred in the production process (excluding one-time costs).

COST OF MATERIALS AND ENERGY RESOURCES SAVING 564189498712 - savings achieved by the implementation of measures to improve the use of material and energy resources.

COSTS OF MAINTENANCE AND OPERATION OF EQUIPMENT 59872149874 - costs, including the following items: depreciation of equipment and vehicles for the movement of labor items, operation of equipment, maintenance, wear and tear of low-value and wear tools and devices, etc.

COST OF PRODUCTION 598471319498 - The aggregate of expenses directly connected to production, rendering of services expressing in monetary terms.

COST OF PRODUCTS 694 731918 849 - current costs of the enterprise for the production and sale of products, expressed in monetary form.

COST REDUCTION FACTORS 498 314219 618 - a system of organizational and technical measures carried out in order to reduce current production costs and sales of products.

COSTS ASSOCIATED WITH ONE MONETARY UNIT OF MARKETABLE PRODUCTS 914918 718 497 – Summarized economical index expressing share of current costs in cost of marketable products.

COSTS REDUCING FACTORS 498 314219 618 – a system of organizational and technical measures undertaken in order to reduce the current costs of production and sales.

COST STRUCTURE 819 671219 78 - the share of current costs for each calculation item in the unit cost or the share of each element of current costs in the total amount of current production costs.

CURRENT SUPPLY 671 814218 17 – a general type of rated stock which determined as product of average daily consumption of objects of production and interval between two deliveries.

COVERAGE RATIO 516 719219 71 – the share of enterprise or industry products in the total production of professional goods.

CREDIT RISK 489 617317 489 - probability of violation of the agreement on the timeliness of payment received on credit for products (services), reduction of revenue when entering the market with new products, etc.

CREDIT TICKET 714819648514 - is a debt obligation that replaces money.

CREDITOR 514 567319 518 - is a legal or natural person who lends, provides a loan for a specified period of time with payment of the interest rate for services to the creditor.

CREDITOR'S DEBT 564812319481 - funds currently attracted by the organization, which are subject to return to the creditor, taking into account the payment of the corresponding interest for the loan received.

CREDITWORTHINESS 498 617218 714 - the ability of a physical or legal entity to fulfill all financial obligations in accordance with the terms of the contract.

CRISIS OF OVERPRODUCTION 4851481619 71 – Circumstances in case of which produced goods do not find supplying because of exceeding against actual needs.

CRITICAL ABSOLUTE FACE-VISIBLE COEFFICIENT 564 719489 471 - is an indicator of the assessment of the financial condition of the enterprise, defined as the ratio of the amount of cash and cash equivalents to short-term liabilities.

CURRENT ACCOUNT 319718904614 – Document, reflecting availability of free funds, temporarily stored in the credit and financial institutions. Used for cash settlement of physical and legal persons.

CURRENT LIQUIDITY COEFFICIENT 619 718498 41 - real provision of the enterprise with working capital (current capital) for normal economic activity under the mandatory condition of timely repayment of the loan and other urgent cash from working capital. It is calculated by the ratio of the value of the working capital of the enterprise to the amount of urgent obligations.

CURRENT ASSETS 371 821498317 – Material and financial resources altogether required for the appropriate functioning of the production process and product sales.

CURRENCY INTERVENTION 317548218716 - entry of the price bank into the foreign exchange market in order to strengthen or lower the exchange rate of the national currency by buying and selling foreign banknotes.

CURRENT SUPPLY 671 814218 17 – A general type of rated stock which determined as product of average daily consumption of objects of production and interval between two deliveries.

CUSTOMER ARREARS 316318819412 - unpaid cost share of goods sold on credit.

CUSTOMS BARRIER 649 749319 74 – establishment by the state of high rates of duties on imported goods in order to limit their supply.

CUSTOMS DUTIES 61721451728 - is a type of state tax that provides for a monetary fee on imported, export and transit goods.

CUSTOMER EXPENDITURES 218 619719 811 – Expenses for transportation and forwarding operations, applying to goods in circulation included customs duties payment, taxes and duties, travel and entertainment expenses and so on.

CURRENT PRODUCTION COSTS 718 648 – a totality of material and labor costs for the manufacture of products. Includes wages of the main production workers, raw materials and materials, purchased products and semi-finished products, depreciation, spare parts for repair, low-value and wear items, fuel, etc.

CURTAILMENTS 319842 197 - state restriction or ban on the use of property.

D

DAILY DEMAND GOODS 319 491298 714 - are consumer goods that the buyer acquires constantly depending on the needs at the time of purchase and sale.

DEALER 564814519712 – Stock exchange member purchasing and selling stock on a voluntary basis on own account.

DEBTOR 319518614217 - is a debtor of an enterprise or firm.

DEBIT 318782614 417 – Left part of balance sheet. Presence of goods and material values, cash means as well as the increase of them are entered on debit of positive accounts. Sources of cash means and the decrease are put to passive accounts debit.

DEBTOR 319518614217 – Debtors of enterprise or firm.

DECLINE IN PRODUCTION 694 218549 714 - is a stage of the product life cycle, when the technical and economic characteristics of the goods do not fully meet the requirements of the consumer, which causes a gradual reduction in the volume of production of this product up to its replacement with a new or modernized one.

DEFICIT 61401568148 – Exceeding demand over supply what is displayed with non-sufficient provision of material values, instruments and subjects of labor, labor force and consumer goods.

DEINDUSTRIALIZATION 614574818471 - is an economic situation reflecting a decrease in the share of industrial production in gross national income.

DELIVERY 819471 - is an agreement obliging the seller to supply the consumer with products and other material values within the prescribed period with a specified volume.

DELIVERY INTERVAL 619718918714 – Period of time between planned deliveries of goods and materials.

DEMAND 518 681319 719 - is an economic category characteristic of commodity production and reflecting the total public need for various goods, taking into account the payment ability of buyers.

DEMAND CURVE 6441818319 481 - is a curve that graphically reflects the law of demand, according to which when the price decreases, demand grows and, conversely, demand falls with price increases.

DEMAND EXCESS 498 712719489 - market circumstances express shortage of goods as consequence of excess of demand over supply.

DEMAND EQUATION 694 713519 498 - is an economic and mathematical model in which demand or demand is a variable depending on changing factors.

DEMAND FORMATION 94218319718 - is a system of organizational and economic measures of the marketing service of the enterprise to ensure the sale of finished products, which is developed on the basis of the results of the analysis of existing markets in order to assess the solvency of potential buyers, the level of competitiveness of its own products and potential opportunities of competitors, satisfaction of the needs and probability

DEMAND FUNCTION 513819719498 - mathematical dependence of demand for various goods and services on such factors as the emergence of substitute goods, an increase in the number of buyers, an increase in their solvency, etc.

DEMAND OVERFLOW 319618 - excessive demand transferred to another market.

DEMAND SATURATION 89731949861 – is a market situation in which prices for many goods and services are sharply reduced, and demand for individual goods falls.

DEMAND SOLVENT 317 498219 641 - change in demand depending on the growth or decrease in income of demanders.

DEMAND-PULL INFLATION 54861421971 – Consequence of aggregate demand exceeding over supply i.e., growth of prices for goods and services which may be acquired at higher prices and tariffs.

DEMAND VALUE 31721851427 - valuation of the quantity of a certain product that can be purchased by the buyer at a set price within a given period of time.

DEMAND VOLUME 479 716 819 41 - the quantity of goods purchased on the market by the consumer.

DEMAND WITH SINGLE ELASTICITY 519 691917 819 - is a market situation in which the rate of demand growth is equal to the rate of price decline or the rate of price growth - the rate of decline in demand.

DEPOSIT 48949131841 - temporary storage of funds and securities in state stressed and commercial financial and credit institutions (commercial and savings banks) and organizations (notarial offices).

DEPOSIT «funds or property» 398628198711 - funds or property that act as means of the enterprise, ensuring the fulfillment of the mandatory conditions fixed in the contract. In case of violation of contractual terms, penalties are imposed.

DEPOSIT INTEREST 519312619712 - is the interest rate paid by the bank on customer deposits.

DEPOSIT «temporarily stored in financial» 319618719814 – funds, shares, promissory notes and other valuables that are temporarily stored in financial and credit institutions and which the depositor (depositor) can dispose of at his discretion.

DEPOSITION «statement» 48949131841 – monetary fund and stock temporary kept in state and commercial credit institutions (commercial and saving banks) and agencies (notary offices).

DEPRECIATION 519318491417 – gradual transfer of the cost of fixed assets to the produced product or service in order to accumulate money for their further full recovery.

DEPRECIATION 498312514 – Loss of goods use value as a result of mechanical utilization or of natural causes influence.

DEPRESSION 564898719612 – stage of breaking or phase of productive cycle followed immediately after economic crisis that is after period of sharp decrease of purchasing demand and of goods output growth (overproduction).

DEPRECIATION FUND 489317519814 – funds intended to replace fixed assets.

DEPRECIATION RATE 48971851947 – share or established rate as a percentage of the book value of the main backgrounds per year.

DEREGULATION 57849861451 – Withdrawal from state supervision.

DESINFLATION 564517 498748 – Falling of inflation level or its full liquidation.

DETERMINIZM 81971488 481 – Form of social development based on science and technology progress.

DEVALUATION 978541 219714 - is a state system of legislative measures that ensures the balance of demand and the supply of the national currency of the country by reviewing its exchange rate downwards in relation to precious metals and the currency of other countries; monetary reform, providing for the withdrawal from circulation of depreciated banknotes and their exchange for full-fledged banknotes.

DEVELOPING MARKETING 498317519641 - is the process of forming demand for goods (services), interest in which is observed in the market, but cannot be satisfied due to the lack of relevant products.

DEVERSIFICATION 498485 48917 - Widening of economic sphere of the enterprise, association or an industry for the purposes of range of product increase and rise of new products share in total production volume what leads to realignment of product strategy for strengthening of commodity market position.

DIFFICULT INTEREST 498 728519 742 - the coefficient used to determine the amount of loan repayment and determine the basis for calculating investment payments.

DIRECT COMMUNICATIONS 518 649319 817 - agreements concluded between manufacturers, consumers and suppliers of inventory, on planned supply of various production resources, finished products and performance of services.

DIRECT COST 564917319817 - strictly targeted expenditures. They are included in prime cost of unit of product by the method of direct calculating; for example, expenses for materials and salaries of production and related workers.

DIRECT TAX 4864728941 - Established by law compulsory payments to the budget, which are levied on the income or property of individuals and legal entities.

DISCOUNT 519617 918489 – Difference between security nominal cost and its selling cost; price reduction (discount) of goods cost.

DISCOUNT «result of changes» 714 824391 68 - the size of a possible decrease in the basic price of goods as a result of changes in market conditions (fall in demand, wholesale, etc.) or the terms of agreement.

DISCOUNT NORM 31864831951 - a temporarily established interest rate for the payment of dividends on shares, deposits, to determine the amount of loan repayment.

DISCOUNT POLICY 519 817498 218 – Policy of financial system targeted on the discount rate for credit.

DISCOUNT RATE 31864831951 – temporarily set the interest rate for the payment of dividends on shares, deposits, to determine the amount of repayment.

DISCOUNTING EXPENDITURES 564 712819 516 - reduction of different time wasting when estimating of investment project efficiency according to time wasting of beginning or ending period on the basis of usage of compound interest.

DISCOVERY 564 714 - is a radical transformation at the level of knowledge based on the identification of new objectively existing patterns of changing the world.

DISINFLATION 564517 498748 - falling inflation or its total elimination.

DISTRIBUTION COST 519 798498 716 – total expenditure of labor and productive means including transportation expenses, storage and etc. expressing in money terms and put on finished product in the course of commodity circulation process.

DISPOSAL OF INDUSTRIAL WASTE 317 498513 471 - processing of industrial waste for further use; one of the directions of increasing the efficiency of the use of material resources.

DIVIDEND 519316 918714 - A share of profit gained by Joint Stock Company over a certain period of time after tax payment, allotment of means for production development, social needs and insurance. The share of profit is liable to distribution among shareholders (owners of stock) according to decision admitted at general meeting of shareholders.

DIVISION OF LABOR 58497131964 - separation of different types of labor activity in the production process.

DOCUMENT CIRCULATION 548 617319714 – Movement of business papers inside of enterprise, firm, institution.

DUMPING 518914319714 – is a type of competition when a large number of goods appear on the market, delivered at artificially low prices, in individual cases below cost; export of goods at lower prices.

DUOPOLY 48942818949 - is a market in which certain products are sold only by two representatives of large industrial monopolistic groups not bound by a price agreement.

DYNAMIC OF CURRENT OUTLAYS 318617 918714 - Dependence of current expenditures on product manufacturing change from production growth or volume decrease.

E

ECONOMIC ACCOUNTING 316819719718 - is a system of constant accounting of the entire set of current and one-time costs associated with the production of products and the performance of services.

ECONOMIC ANNUAL EFFECT 519 618219 717 - is the result of economic activity, which is calculated based on the compared options for capital investment and represents the difference between the reduced costs adjusted for annual production.

ECONOMIC BLOCKADE 71851781914 - economic isolation carried out in order to curb the development of the economic activities of any state.

ECONOMIC CATEGORY 69831821971 - is a theoretical expression of the main aspects of production relations that develop in the process of creating material goods, their sale and consumption.

ECONOMIC EFFECT 598 671291 649 - is the result of the implementation of an appropriate measure, which can be expressed by savings from cost reduction, profit, with an increase in profit or national income, etc.

ECONOMIC EFFICIENCY ABSOLUTE (GENERAL) 316518498917 - effectiveness of capital investments in the national economy, economic district, industry, construction of new and reconstruction of existing enterprises, etc.

ECONOMIC EFFICIENCY COMPARATIVE 514289598617- is an indicator that is used in choosing the best option for solving an economic problem.

ECONOMIC EFFICIENCY OF CAPITAL INVESTMENTS 518317219491 - is an indicator reflecting the feasibility of implementing one-time costs, which is based on a measurement of the resulting effect (eco-action, profit, etc.) and capital investments that ensured this result.

ECONOMIC EFFICIENCY OF NEW TECHNOLOGY 518316498217 - is the result of the introduction of scientific and technological progress, combined with the capital expenditures for the implementation of this event.

ECONOMIC EFFICIENCY OF THE INVESTMENT PROJECT 614212319491 - the effectiveness of the investment project.

ECONOMIC EQUILIBRIUM 519819491712 - is a hypothetical situation in the market, when there is an identity of products and supply to the goods available on the market.

ECONOMIC LOGISTICS 518317216498 - economic assessment of each of the stages (stages) of promotion of material flows (information, etc.), from the purchase of raw materials and materials to ensure production processes and up to the transportation of finished products to the place of sale.

ECONOMIC REGULATORS 498481919 47 - a set of state calculations to influence the economy (taxes, interest rates, etc.).

ECONOMIC WARFARE 71851781914 – Economic isolation carried out for the purposes of suppression of any country economic activity development.

ECONOMIC POLICY 694318219718 - a set of organizational and management measures of economic development, developed and approved to achieve goals and objectives at various levels of management, ranging from the enterprise (improving the level of competitiveness of production and goods) to the government level (national and investment policy, etc.).

ECONOMY 519318498614 - is a scientific discipline that studies the processes of economic activity of the enterprise (microeconomics), industries (mesoeconomics), large-scale economic phenomena and processes - inflation, employment level, etc. (macroeconomics).

ECONOMY MODE 518497219614 - is a set of organizational and technical measures aimed at improving production efficiency through rational use of labor and material resources of production, eliminating over-planned downtime of equipment.

ECONOMY SURVIVABILITY 564317319818 – stable economic position of the state carried out its policy purposefully under influence of any external and internal social economic conditions.

EFICACIA DE ASIGNACIÓN (ALLOCATIVE EFFICIENCY) 561418519471 - la distribución más racional de los recursos naturales en dirección hacia su uso final.

EFFECTIVE MARKET 698 721319 78 - is a condition that ensures an immediate response to market prices.

EFFECTIVE TIME FUND (VALID) 614 212318 617 - useful time used during the planned period.

ELASTICITY COEFFICIENT 518 619419 714 - a significant change in the quantity of goods sold, which accounts for one percent of the change in the price of the goods (product).

ELASTICITY OF DEMAND 516 718219 614 - ratio of changes in price and demand for goods.

ELASTICITY OF THE OFFER 498 614219 718 - correlation of changes in sales volume and price of goods.

ENERGY ARMEDNESS OF LABOR 714 728519 618 - is a device reflecting the power of the corresponding energy carriers per average worker.

ENERGY RESOURCES 61931851964 - a set of all types of energy and energy carriers (power machines, transformer devices and other energy carriers used for the production and distribution of energy at the enterprise), providing the production process and other energy needs (lighting, heating, etc.).

ENGINEERING 516318514217 – Sphere of commercial organization (company) activity for provision of engineering consulting services in production organizing and sales of product for entities (enterprises) of production industry and another economical industry.

ENTREPRENEURSHIP 71974131981 - is an independent activity of individuals or legal entities aimed at generating income, maximum profit from the sale of goods, performance of works, provision of services.

ENTERPRISE 47131951841 - is an independent economic entity endowed with the rights of a legal entity and using its own or leased production facilities that ensure the production and sale of products (services) to meet the needs of society and make a profit.

ENTERPRISE (FIRM) LIQUIDATION 61481481247 – Termination of enterprise (firm) activity on the basis of court decision on finding of insolvency, according to elapsed time which was assigned for its running, because of general meeting resolution (for JSC), superior body (for state enterprises).

ENTERPRISE (FIRM) LIQUIDITY 516814514817 – Firm capability to timely discharge loan debt.

ENTERPRISE LIFE CYCLE 819714319612 – Economically justified period of the enterprise commercial activity.

ENTERPRISE PROPERTY TAX 49871271941 - fixed assets, intangible assets, stocks and expenses on the payer's balance sheet are taxed.

ENTERPRISE'S WORKING CAPITALS TURNOVER 498 617498714 - Includes stages: at first stage working capital transit from monetary form to commodity form (production stock and labor force are acquitted), at second stage production inventory through the use of labor force and labor instruments converts into finished product; at third stage finished product is sold, means disengage from the commodity form for becoming monetary one.

EQUIPMENT 371 498 271 47 - is an integral part of fixed assets, including tools used for direct impact on the subject of labor.

EQUIPMENT LOADING 518671319148 - intra-shift time utilization factor reflecting the share of the actual operating time of the equipment during a certain period (shift, day, decade, etc.) in the total effective fund of time of the installed equipment for the corresponding period. Products, semi-finished products, fuel) and other elements of the working capital that are in the warehouse of the enterprise, but have not yet been put into technological processing.

EQUILIBRIUM ECONOMIC 89562131949 - is a market situation in which the needs of buyers coincide with the plans of sellers, i.e., at this price of goods there is a balance of supply and demand.

EQUIPMENT CAPACITY 648517 - is the reverse indicator of equipment utilization.

EQUIPMENT DOWNTIME 981498714317 - inactivity of equipment during working hours.

EQUILIBRIUM MARKET 54847981971 - is an economic situation in the market in which the value of demand is equal to the value of supply.

EQUIPMENT NEED 571481498 - quantitative assessment of the need for equipment to fulfill the planned volume of production (for a month, quarter, year).

EQUIPMENT OPERATING TIME FUND 619714219611 - is a calendar working time fund of a unit of equipment, calculated as a product of the number of calendar days in a year, quarter, month, decade.

EQUIPMENT OPERATING TIME FUNDS «multiplied by 24 hours» 489891318514 - includes a calendar fund (i.e., the number of calendar days per year multiplied by 24 hours).

EQUIPMENT PARK 319516818317 - a list of equipment on the balance sheet of the enterprise. There are no many types of equipment park: basic technological, installed, auxiliary, etc.

EQUIPMENT PARK UPDATE 671 49881 - replacement of physically worn and obsolete equipment with a newer and more productive one.

EQUIPMENT PRODUCTIVITY 49871489811 - an indicator characterizing the processing time of a set of parts on compared models of interchangeable equipment.

EQUIPMENT REPLACEMENT EFFICIENCY 319 618219 718 - in addition to reducing the average age of equipment and increasing the annual effective fund of equipment operating time, provides an increase in the share of advanced equipment, and therefore the technical level of production.

ESTIMATED COST OF CONSTRUCTION 519 648518 742 - costs necessary for the construction and commissioning of the main production facilities according to the approved project.

ESTIMATE OF COSTS FOR MAINTENANCE AND OPERATION OF EQUIPMENT 219 317498 648 - estimate including the following cost items: depreciation of equipment and transport vehicles; operation and maintenance of equipment and vehicles; in-plant transportation of goods; wear of low-value and wear tools, devices, etc.

ESTIMATE OF COSTS FOR PREPARATION AND DEVELOPMENT OF PRODUCTION 548 671319 894 - an estimate that is made for newly developed products or technology for each division of the enterprise, and then consolidated into a single estimate with a decoding of costs for calculation items and cost elements.

ESTIMATE OF GENERAL PLANT EXPENSES 548 648319 712 - estimate, including the costs of enterprise management (the salary of the management apparatus, business trip and transfer, maintenance of fire and paramilitary security; general expenses, etc.).

ESTIMATE OF INCOME AND EXPENSES 498 718519 647 - a document reflecting the amount of upcoming income and expenses.

ESTIMATE OF NON-PRODUCTION COSTS 894 716219 418 - summary of costs for packaging, packaging, transportation of finished products, commission deductions to sales organizations, etc.

ESTIMATE OF WORKSHOP COSTS 514 917219 814 - estimate including the following items: maintenance of the workshop management apparatus and other personnel; depreciation of buildings and structures, inventory; expenses for testing, experiments, investigations, labor protection; wear and tear of low-wearing equipment.

EVALUATION OF THE MAIN PRODUCTION FUNDS 614813519714 - methods used to assess the replacement value, i.e., the value that reflects the time required to reproduce the goods in modern conditions.

EVIQUATION 514318485497 - court decision to transfer the acquired property to the actual owner due to the fact that the seller did not have the legal right to sell it.

ETERPRISE'S ECONOMY DESTABILISATION 519814519711 – Evaluation of technical and economic opportunities for achievement of manufacturer and consumer interests' concordance.

EXCISES 518716319419819 - are a type of indirect taxes, which are an integral part of the selling price and are fully deducted to the budget. They are mainly installed on consumer goods.

EXCCESS RESERVE 619 712719 819 – Supernormal commodity stock and supplies which influence on decrease of working capital efficacy.

EXCESS OF PRODUCTION POWERFULLNESS 519 617319418 – excess of potential possibility of product manufacturing over actual output.

EXCESS OF SUPPLY 489 817497498 - overstocking as a result of excess of supply over demand.

EXCLUSIVE IMPLEMENTATION 69849131971 - the realization by the manufacturer of its own products in a particular market through a single representative of wholesale or retail trade.

EXCHANGE 689714891491 - is a form of a permanent system of purchase and sale on the basis of a bilateral agreement.

EXCHANGE DEAL 487198598641 - Direct cashless exchange of goods. General cause of exchange deal is currency and cash means problems.

EXCHANGE MARKET INTERVENTION 317548218716 - a central bank entry into a foreign exchange market for the purposes of strengthening and exchange rate decrease of national currency.

EXCHANGE RATE 18942149718516 - the number of currency or monetary units of one country required to acquire a monetary unit of another country.

EXHIBITION FAIR 714182689411 - periodically arranged showing of achievements in different industries.

EXPENSES FOR DEVELOPMENT AND PREPARATION OF PRODUCTION 49857189464 - costs, which include costs for the development of new enterprises, workshops, new types of products and technological processes; for design and design, development of the technological process of manufacturing a new product; for redevelopment, rearrangement and adjustment of equipment, etc.

EXPANSION OF DEMAND 4853131947 - increase in demand for consumer goods as a result of growth in population or per capita income.

EXPANSION OF SALES MARKETS 74931721978 - development of an action plan to increase the sale of goods through introduction to new markets.

EXPENSES OF FUTURE PERIODS 3174895196 - costs incurred in relevant future periods.

EXPENDITURES 319 718519 612 - Expenses sum expressing in monetary terms and implemented for manufacturing and sales of product and rendering of services.

EXPEDITIONARY INTERMEDIARY 498 491319 81 - a legal entity carrying out on the basis of concluded contracts.

EXPORT OF CAPITAL FROM THE COUNTRY 548219618717 - Advancing of monetary means for oversees business organizing.

EXTRA CHARGE 69831721941 - artificial increase of price to pay to procurement agencies; agreed surcharge for the fulfillment of the commodity producer (supplier) additional requirements of the buyer.

FACTORS OF PRODUCTION 519 471218 614 - the main elements of the production stage of creation of material goods and services (products of production, labor resources, etc.).

FACTORS OF LABOR PRODUCTIVITY GROWTH 718 649317 713 - qualitative and quantitative changes in the organization of material production, ensuring the growth of labor productivity.

FAIR 516 218319 712 - is a type of periodically functioning market for the sale of means of production, consumer goods and services.

FALSE BANKRAPTCY 219 471 91 – inappropriate information of a legal entity on refusal to pay on its debt obligations on the basis of fictitious reason.

FEASIBILITY STUDY 5980750171 319891 - confirmation of the feasibility of implementing the proposed construction project, technical transfer of weapons, reconstruction of the enterprise, etc.

FINANCE OF THE ENTERPRISE (FIRM) 514318319418 - is a system of financial and economic relations that arise in the process of the cycle of fixed assets and working capital in the field of production and circulation.

FINANCIAL ANALYSIS 598492564317 - study of the directions of ensuring the sustainability of the financial situation of the enterprise.

FINANCING 578 491319 641 - the activity of the enterprise, the company, aimed at ensuring the financial resources of the needs for one-time and current costs.

FINANCIAL CONTROL 319 648218 714 - control over the activities of the company (enterprise) by the bank, which is carried out on the basis of the use of planned cost indicators and covers the production, distribution, processing and consumption of inventory in monetary terms.

FINANCIAL BLOCKADE5 519 618558 19 – is a system of measures aimed at reducing or stopping export rates, eliminating preferential terms of insurance, credit and financial and credit institutions of the state or group of countries against another state.

FINANCIAL FLOW 491 516218 614 - movement of monetary (financial) funds, which act as a logistics system of financial and economic relations in the process of promoting inventory and intangible values (services, working capital, intangible assets, etc.).

FINANCIAL PLAN 485 461319 618 - is a plan that reflects in monetary form the balance of income and expenses, as well as the financial results of the enterprise (firm).

FINANCIAL RESOURCES 71964851978 - monetary funds that are the property of the state, enterprises, organizations and other legal entities and individuals.

FINANCIAL REPORT 219,816 - reporting form that includes the company's total balance sheet; profit and loss statement.

FINISHED PRODUCT 49148189816 – Passed through all technology stages of production process and accepted by quality control department for sales product which meets established standards and technical specification.

FINISHED PRODUCTS «assembly and control» 59871249821 - products that have undergone all technological operations (including assembly and control), completed in production in accordance with established standards or specifications and delivered to the warehouse for sale.

FINISHED PRODUCT STANDARD 39861429871 - time for gathering, packaging, assemblage of products up to the transiting norms, shipping, etc., in terms of value, the need for working capital for the storage of finished products.

FINISHED WORK 368214289716 - products that have not passed all technological operations.

FIRM CAPABILITY 598782614016 - Business plan division presented general branches of firm productive activity with notification of aims (production and sales volumes, revenue and benefit provision and increase of firm production (services) market share) and organization technical measures for the accomplishing.

FIRM OFFER 548 671571 498 41 - the offer of the manufacturer (seller) for the sale of a certain product pair, which is valid until a response is received from the buyer's side and does not allow us to offer this product to other buyers.

FIXED ASSETS IN USE 519317498516481 - integral and key part of fixed production assets which serves as basis for evaluation of technical level for manufacturing capacity.

FIXED PAYMENTS 719 748219 642 - mandatory payments to the budget of part of the profit, the increase of which is not related to the use of production reserves, but is the result of budget allocations for the development of the enterprise, firm.

FLEXIBILITY 548578914216 - Presence of different organization opportunities to rearrange fast for changed circumstances of economic activity.

FLEXIBILITY IN PLANNING 319781894216 - Adjustment of intra productive plans with due account for internal and external changed production circumstances, which allows to update planning directions and to provide production continuity.

FLEXIBLE TECHNOLOGY 517891619318 - Ability of provided technology to rearrange fast for changed circumstances of economic activity.

FLOATING INTEREST RATE 719316319481 - is loan interest on term and long-term loans, the amount of which is non-permanent and is periodically revised by agreement between the lender and the borrower at established intervals or at the request of one of the parties.

FISCAL INCOME 516481319471 - results of the activity of fiscal monopolies, which have a mono-full right to produce and trade in certain goods (wine and water, tobacco products).

FISCAL POLICY 51831949871 - state policy in the field of taxation and formation of revenue and expenditure parts of the state budget.

FIRM 47131421981 - is an industrial, commercial or economic enterprise endowed with the rights of a legal entity.

FONDO DE AMORTIZACIÓN (SINKING FUND) 489317519814 – Dinero destinado a la sustitución de activos fijos.

FRANCO 498319519451 - distribution of transport goods during the purchase and sale (delivery) of goods.

FREEDOM OF ENTERPRISE ZONE 914518564 912 - state territory.

FREIGHT 498513219714 - payment for transportation of inventory or passengers by water. Charged after transportation.

FREIGHT TURNOVER 59418739861 - Economic indicator expressing work made by freight transportation. It is calculated as the weight of freight transported over a certain period multiplied by the distance of transportation.

FREE CONTRACT PRICE 514 697894 798 - price formed on a contractual basis between the manufacturer (seller) and the buyer working in a market relation.

FUEL AND ENERGY COMPLEX 618 317219 489 - is a set of enterprises of various industries producing and processing fuel and energy resources.

FUEL AND ENERGY RESOURCES FOR TECHNOLOGICAL PURPOSES 619 518498 717 - cost item, which reflects the current costs of fuel for foundry production and heating of metal in the forging and pressing shop, the cost of energy for electric furnaces, technological equipment, lighting, heating, etc.

FUND CAPACITY INCREASE 319718219614 - is an indicator that is used in assessing the impact of various factors on the level of use of fixed assets in the study period.

FUNDS IN CALCULATIONS 548 614819 714 - temporarily withdrawn funds of the enterprise for settlement with physical and legal entities.

FUNDS IN GOODS SHIPPED 54831941948 - part of the irregular working capital that is shipped to the consumer without advance payment, i.e., the consumer transfers funds for shipped products to the manufacturer's account after receipt of the goods.

FUND OF CALENDAR TIME 584319489417 – Potential time of equipment work over a year.

FUND RETURN 317518614217 - is a general indicator that reveals the use of fixed assets.

FUND RETURN ACTIVE 319317219498 - fund return, which is calculated not for the entire cost of fixed production funds, but only by the cost of their active part.

FUND RETURN INDEX 618517219418 - is an indicator that reflects the change in fund return in the following year compared to the previous one.

FUNDAMENTAL RESEARCH 514212819471 - is the direction of scientific research engaged in the study of objective regularities of the development of nature, society, production forces and the creation of a scientific base for the design of new equipment, technology, etc.

FUNCTIONAL ORGANIZATION OF MAR-KETING DEPARTMENTS 618317819498 - providing advertising of products and services, stimulating the sale of finished products and branding research.

G

GENERAL LAW OF LABOR PRODUCTIVITY GROWTH 518671319489 - reflects the result of the introduction of more advanced and productive tools, the use of which reduces the labor intensity of a unit of product and wage savings (release of live labor) with an increase in depreciation (past labor). Their increase is also recorded in the debit of active accounts, cash statements and their reduction - in the debit of passive accounts.

GENERAL LEASING 317514818417 - agreement for lease in which lessee is provided with right of equipment stock (machines, devices etc.) replenishment as per leasing without additional agreement of firm-lessor.

GENERAL PLANT EXPENSES 671 674891 712 - costs associated with the management and organization of enterprise production.

GLOBAL PREFERENTIAL SYSTEM 491719 819481 - Customs privileges which are given to under-developed and developing countries.

GLOBALIZATION 31968971921 – New process of mutual economic development of the world countries directed to world market demand satisfaction on the basis of exchange of international economic activity results when material and spiritual values accomplishing plays a part of a constituent of world production.

GOODS DISTRIBUTION CHANNEL 61949831947 – Consequence of goods carrying forward from a manufacturer to a consumer.

GOVERNMENT CONTRACTUAL WORK 648417918217 – type of cooperation between the government and an enterprise. State is construed as principal and guarantees a payment for product manufacturing to the enterprise.

GOVERNMENTAL BUDGET 598618517544 – balance list of income and expenses developed, approved and regulated by legislative and executive organs of authority.

GROSS DOMESTIC PRODUCT (GDP) 189014 918715 – an economic indicator reflecting the total cost of the final product (goods and services) created in the country for a certain period.

GROSS INCOME 516318 – is the total result of the activity of the enterprise, the company, which includes revenue from the sale of products, the liquidation value of the withdrawn property, income from non-industrial economic activity.

GROSS NATIONAL PRODUCT (GDP) 914815316498 – is an economic indicator reflecting the market The value of the final (finished) product produced by the country during the year.

GROSS PRODUCTS 317148648141 – is a cost-nomic indicator that reflects in monetary terms the total volume of products produced for a certain period (month, quarter, year), excluding value added tax.

GROSS PUBLIC PRODUCT (VOP) 421516318714 - the cost of the annual volume of products produced in the field of material production.

GROSS SOCIAL PRODUCT (GNP) 421516318714 - cost of yearly volume of product manufactured in the sphere of material production.

GROWTH FACTOR OF THE MAIN PRODUCTION FUNDS 518 614219714 - is a coefficient defined as the ratio of the increase in the value of fixed assets of their value at the end of the year.

GROWTH RATE OF PRODUCTION 518 671 819 491 - the ratio of the actual cost of manufactured products and services rendered to the planned value or the ratio of the total cost of the next year to the previous one.

GROWTH OF PRODUCTION VOLUME 819712498 478 - is a stage of the product life cycle, which is characterized by an increase in the production of a certain product (goods) due to the growth of demand.

H

HEDGING 498516319714 - insurance of risk associated with changes in prices, exchange rates, shares.

HIDDEN UNEMPLOYMENT 648 217214 81 - is an economic situation in which part of the able-bodied population is only formally listed on the list of workers, but neither directly nor directly participates indirectly in the creation of material goods.

HIRING 491516319318 - medium-term lease agreement (from one year to five years); one of the forms of leasing.

HIRINGER 371491 - is one of the parties to the hiring, which provides the hiring user with property for temporary use for monetary remuneration.

HOLDING COMPANY 498516219478 - is a joint-stock company that owns a controlling stake in other legal entities and controls their activities and distribution of income in the form of dividends.

HOMOGENEOUS GOODS 514 812719 61 - goods (products) sold on the market by various producers as analogues or substitutes that do not have preference.

I

INCREASE IN LABOR PRODUCTIVITY 54848131941 - an economic indicator determined on the basis of a reduction in the number of workers or employees.

INVESTMENT POLICY 219 716218714 – Integrity of socio-economical measures that allows defining of priority branches of capital investment in different industries.

IMAGE 48948919141 – Reputation, public evaluation of enterprise activity formed for clients and suppliers, consumers and so on.

IMBALANCE 514219318718 – Notion vice versa to deficit, i.e., actual value exceeded over calculated or planned.

IMMOBILIZATION OF WORKING CAPITAL 219618 214 – Extraction of part of working capital from production process for out of planning measures under conditions of following use as it was primarily intended.

IMPLEMENTATION STRATEGY 548 748919 216 - is the process of attracting buyers and gaining a certain market share by using lower prices compared to analogues presented by competitors.

INCOME 589317318614 – monetary means, material values, getting by corporate bodies and individuals as commission for rendering services. This kind of income is typical for non-productive sphere (trade, banking, exchanges, transport, communications and so on).

INCOME EFFECT 518 617219 71 - change in the real progress of the buyer as a result of an increase or decrease in price.

INCOME TAX 491819317481 - is a component of the balance sheet profit, which serves as a source of redistribution of national income.

INCOME TAX « main type of direct ta» 42851748948 - is the main type of direct tax, which is levied on the income or profit of the enterprise and goes to the revenue part of the budget.

INCOMPARABLE PRODUCTS 589712698714 - products developed in the current period, as well as products of pilot production produced in the previous year and products for which changes in technical specifications are provided.

INCOMPLETE PRODUCTION 594817319714 – partly finished products, not fully passed all technological operations provided by production specifications of the finished product.

INCREMENT RATE OF ECONOMY 514 916317 819 –The reduction in growth of costs attributed to the value of the gain in production volume.

INCREMENT RATE OF FIXED PRODUCTION ASSETS 518 614219714 – ratio, defined as the ratio of increase in the value of fixed assets to their value at the end of the year.

INCREASE FUND INTENSITY FACTOR 519618 94 - is an indicator calculated as the ratio of the growth of fixed assets to the increase in production as a RESULT of an increase in materialized capital investments for a certain period (month, quarter, year).

INCREASE IN LABOR PRODUCTIVITY 54848131941 - an economic indicator determined on the basis of a reduction in the number of workers or employees.

INDEXATION 514821619317 – Correction of private income for the purposes of reimbursement of monetary loss and keeping of actual value of income under conditions of inflation accompanied by price growth.

INDICATIVE PLANNING 619718519711 – Variety of state economy planning which is regularly used for economy crisis weakening, elimination of its consequences, rise of commercial production level, decrease of unemployment, regulation of market economy and so on.

INDIRECT TAX 42131931781 - tax on goods and services, which is established in the form of allowances to the prices of goods or tariffs for services.

INDICATOR 518614219621 – Economic and statistic parameter estimating changes in the course of economic process on the whole and relative to separate constituents of it.

INDICATOR OF CAPITAL INVESTMENTS RECOUPMENT 489 714819 714 – indicator of the period during which the advanced capital investments pay off by savings or profits derived from the materialization of investments.

INDICATOR OF CONSUMER AND RETALE PRICES 319618519412 – Monthly published index describing the changes (dynamics) of cost of set of goods and services rendering towards this area population needs of first turn (consumer basket) satisfying, and of middle level of prices in retail market.

INDICATOR OF ENTRY OR RENOVATION OF BASIC PRODUCTION ASSETS 598 491719 617 – indicator defined as the ratio of the value of the newly introduced basic production assets during the year to their value at the end of the year.

INDICATOR OF EQUIPMENT USAGE (MACHINE UTILIZATION) IN ONE SHIFT OPERATING 619 712319 714 - Indicator of market economy expressing the consumer properties' changing dynamics for goods as a result of carrying out of different organizing technical events and economic factors influence.

Indicator of the intensity of equipment uses, defined as the ratio in which the numerator is a sum each term of which is the product of dimensional interval of a part by load factor of machine with parts of the interval, and the denominator is the product of one of the dimensional parameters of the machine by a factor of the machine utilization.

INDICATOR OF UTILIZATION OF EQUIPMENT SHIFT MODE WORK 421 478561 471 - Ratio of actual indicator of interchangeability to shift mode work of equipment.

INDICATOR OF WORKABILITY FOR EQUIPMENT 518 642198 487 - Indicator characterizing the share of the residual value attributed to 1 monetary unit of equipment prime cost.

INDICATOR OF YIELD OF CAPITAL INVESTMENT 618517219418 - Indicator expressing change of funds' yield in the next year in comparison with the value for the previous.

INDUSTRIAL CAPITAL 564851619471 - Monetary capital advanced to the sphere of material production.

INDUSTRIAL PRODUCTION MANAGEMENT 519 617218 419 - development and use of a management mechanism to ensure the process of normal functioning of production and sale of finished products (services), taking into account the rational use of material, labor and financial resources, comparison of the results of economic activities of the enterprise with costs.

INDUSTRY STRUCTURE 318 492819 714 - classification of economic activities of industrial enterprises by industry or complex industries.

INDUSTRIALIZATION 518671319712 – Process of large-scale machine production development in public economy, first at the industries where labor instruments and subjects of labor are making.

INELASTIC DEMAND 564814319583 – Situation in which the proceeds from the sale of large volume of the goods does not cover losses from the reduction in its price.

INFORMATION FLOW 498648498711 – Instrument of logistic system through the use of which data base is created for satisfaction of particular needs.

INFLATER 56421721849 – Index of price growth.

INFLATION 58421721941 – Monetary depreciation taking place under conditions of monetary mass emission over actual needs which happens in terms of prices growth for goods and services.

INFLATION THRESHOLD 341 617519 81 - the previous inflation rate.

INFLATION RISK 64851731849 – Probability of losses occurrence as a result of price growth.

INFORMATION LETTER 319 317498641 - a letter informing another enterprise or interested person about the fait accompli or about the planned event.

INFORMATION SCIENCE 316849319712 - Discipline to study information structure and properties, laws and methods for its creation, storage, searching, handover and utilization in different spheres of human beings.

INFRASTRUCTURE 598689319718 – complex of branches, enterprises and institutions including in these branches which fulfills functions of commercial and agricultural production service and creates appropriate conditions for operating of a production process and life-sustaining activity of people.

INITIAL COST 51421961871 - the cost of purchasing tools (price), including transportation and installation costs; for capital construction - estimated cost.

IN-LINE EQUIPMENT BASE UTILIZATION INDICATOR 498 671219 714 – indicator defined as the ratio of the quantity of equipment used in the process to the quantity of included in in-line base equipment.

IN-LINE INSTALLED EQUIPMENT BASE UTILIZATION INDICATOR 594 617219 718 - ratio defined as the ratio of the quantity of operating equipment to the number of installed equipment in the shops of the main production or in the enterprise on the whole.

INNOVATION 819418 – Innovations in area of technique, technology, labor and management based on scientific advance and forward experience utilizing.

INNOVATION ACTIVITY 519489619671 – Indicator expressing rate of development, range and continuity of development and implementation of innovations on the basis of scientific advance and forward experience utilization.

INNOVATION POTENTIAL 219016514218 – Technical economic opportunities of production enterprise to design and to produce new competitive product that meets the requirements of the market.

INNOVATION PROJECT 51631851981 – File of documents expressing process of targeted change in technical system on the basis of scientific advance and transition from one economic and technical condition to another more perfect as a result of this system.

INSOLVENCY 48972131971 – Financial position of the persons or entities in which they are not able to meet their financial obligations to pay for goods (services) or to repay debt.

INSOLVENCY 316548319714 - recognized by the state body the lack of payment ability of the debtor to fully satisfy the claims of creditors on monetary obligations or to fulfill the obligation to pay mandatory state payments.

INSURANCE 497 194849 641 - formation of an insurance fund at the expense of contributions from insured legal entities and individuals to compensate for losses of the insured.

INSURANCE RESERVES 564 712819 49 - stocks that are built in case of late receipt of current reserves, i.e., when the actual interval between the two deliveries is greater than planned.

INSPECTION AS A FUNCTION OF ENTERPRISE MANAGEMENT 648 218548 714 – Evaluation of enterprise working results' concordance to regulations' requirements for performance of qualitative and quantitative indicators of socio-economic development.

INSTALLMENT 697518918514 - form of payment for goods (services) in parts.

INSTALLED EQUIPMENT 549 318564 714 - machines, machines and other equipment put into operation and fixed in the workplace, as well as equipment under repair, even if it is temporarily dismantled.

INSOLVENCY 48972131971 - is the financial situation of individuals or legal entities in which they are unable to fulfill their financial obligations to pay for goods (services) or repay debts in a timely manner.

INSTITUTIONAL ECONOMY 56482149871 - Branch of economic science exploration towards reasons of misbalance of system and structural change in sphere of economic relations.

INTEGRAL COEFFICIENT OF EQUIPMENT USE 516219519711 – Economic indicator expressing utilization of equipment work over a shift on the whole and in the frame of shift time.

INTEGRAL EFFECT 514819489471 – Indicator of investment project efficacy estimate presented as aggregate of current effects over a period of calculation on the whole reduced by first year of investment performance.

INTEREST RATE 548317219479 - rate for using a loan.

INTELLECTUAL PROPERTY LAW 491317 - is the legalized right of a legal entity or individual to solely dispose of the results of intellectual property (copyright, patent, etc.).

INTERNAL PRODUCTION (INTRA-FIRM) PLANNING 614812798514 - development of plans for the current work and development of the enterprise, providing for ensuring the planned level of production efficiency on the basis of attracting and rational use of means of production and labor.

INTELLECTUAL INVESTMENTS 519613319819 – Monetary means advanced for scientific researches, licenses, know-how, specialists' training and etc.

INTELLECTUAL PLACEMENT OF FUNDS 316 819319471 – Long term investments aimed at science development, skillful personal training, implementation of scientific technology progress and so on.

INTELLECTUAL PROPERTY 49871271948 – Special form of property expressing possession of rights in results of intellectual labor, right of possession which belongs to authors created the intellectual property, for instance copyright for texts of derivations, design, audio and video work and etc.

INTELLECTUAL PROPERTY LAW 491317 - is the legalized right of a legal entity or individual to solely dispose of the results of intellectual property (copyright, patent, etc.).

INTELLECTUAL WEAR 497189519491 - Process of depreciation of basic capital elements connected to introduction of cheaper and more productive equipment.

INTELLIGENCE QUOTENT 514 214819 714 - an indicator of the level of mental capacity or of the available knowledge. It is based on the use of a specific set of tests.

INTENCIFICATION 564812319712 - Increase of performance as a result of equipment (labor instruments) use improvement towards time and power, rational utilization of material and labor resources.

INTENCITY OF LABOR 584817319714 - Stressfulness of work, aggregate of all energy spending of employee per time unit provided higher labor result.

INTENSIVE IMPLEMENTATION 3986497851 - sale of goods of everyday demand, which the commodity manufacturer realizes through all possible outlets provided by the demand for these products.

INTERMEDIARY 619 71101 8 - is an individual or legal entity assisting in the purchase and sale transaction between the manufacturer and the buyer.

INTERDEPENDENCY OF MARKET 378491819161 - Economic circumstances when one manufacturer product competitive quality growth directly influences on reducing of another sold the same product manufacturer revenue.

INTERNAL EFFICIENCY OF RETURN ON INVESTMENTS 498714898175 - discount rate through the use of which future cash flows discounted value equals a general aggregate investment advanced for the project.

INVENTORY 518 671294 498 - finished products prepared for sale and in the field of commodity circulation, i.e., in stock, on the road, etc.

INVENTORY 478 491 718 498 – material values, working capital (raw materials, materials, equipment and other productive assets) that are sufficient for provision of constant production process.

INVENTORY 481498319712 – Evaluation for each element of presented goods material values of enterprise or their residues on certain date.

INVENTORY HOLDINGS STOCK 598 948714 971 – Most important task of planning especially under conditions of mass serial production is to be defined by quantity of backlog.

INVENTORY RISK 498 714219 489 – Losses which may arise as a result of depreciation of inventory holdings because of prices decrease and intellectual wear of the product.

INVESTMENT BANK 319491819498 - is a bank that issues loan and invests in fixed assets; plays an active role in the issue and placement of investor shares.

INVESTMENT COEFFICIENT 518314319812 - is a coefficient reflecting the share of the country's national income (the main form of accumulation for extended reproduction of fixed assets).

INVESTMENT COMPANY 694318489485 – Financial intermediary accumulating private depositors' monetary means which are used in the sequel for investment implementations for corporate bodies, issuing of own securities and converting them into stocks and shares of other companies.

INVESTMENT FUND 519318614217 - is an open-type credit and financial joint-stock fund that issues its own shares to attract funds from private companies.

INVESTMENT INDICATOR 518314319812 - Indicator expressing share of state national income (fundamental form of accumulation for expanded reproduction of basic production assets).

INVESTMENT INTENCIFICATION 514218519317 - Increase of specific capital contributions related to one average staff member on the basis of scientific and technological advance.

INVESTMENT PAYBACK PERIOD 549 648219 717 - the period required to repay the loan, taking into account the interest rate due to the profit received from the introduction of an advance loan.

INVESTMENT PROJECT ACCEPTANCE 548712317491 - Positive balance of collected actual cash means in any time interval in which given participant makes expenditures or receives income.

INVESTMENT RISKS 514516319718 - the possibility of unforeseen costs and losses in results as a result of uncertainty in the economic situation.

INVESTMENTS 319 617319814 - Long term capital investments in different industries for the purposes of benefit getting.

INVESTOR 618317914217 - is a legal or natural person who carries out long-term investments in an investment project in order to make a profit.

J

JOINT PROPOSAL 614 482318 614 - is an economic situation that reflects the close connection of one product with another. For example, an increase in demand for cameras will lead to an increase in demand for photographic films.

JOINT STOCK COMPANY (JSC) 5163184101482 - is an organizational form of concentration of capital of enterprises, legal entities and citizens, which is the basis for the formation of the authorized capital by issuing and selling securities (shares, bonds, etc.) JSC works in order to create fixed assets (fixed capital) and working capital (current capital).

JOINT VENTURE 649 724319 811 - is a form of organization management structure that does not exclude the participation of foreign partners. The goal is to develop material production and scientific and technical activities.

K

KEYNESIANISM 489421319648 – Theoretical basis for regulations of developed industrial countries and conditions of economic stability support for them.

KINDS OF MERCHANDISE AND SERVICES 619371819481 – Business plan division presented all list of fulfilled products (services) which will be offered for sales in the goods market.

KNOW-HOW 6981831974 – is the result of intellectual work, materialized in scientific and technical solutions that are used in technological processes and ensure the competitiveness of products and increased production efficiency.

L

LABOR 649 714819 217 - is a purposeful activity of the able-bodied population, providing for the creation of material assets and the provision of services with the help of means of production.

LABOR COSTS 58979289431 - expenses, which include basic payments to certain categories of workers.

LABOR EFFECT 519 649319 718 - change in real reach due to pricing.

LABOR EXCHANGE 719481519016 – is a state organization whose work is aimed at meeting the need for labor resources through wide dissemination of the information about the availability of vacancies.

LABOR FORCE MIGRATION 61971549871 - Movement of the able-bodied population as a result of changes in the economic situation in places of labor application.

LABOR FORCE RELEASE 618712319412 – Result of production recession, scientific and technological progress implementation.

LABOR FUND 31961421971 - the average annual value of fixed assets, which comes for one average employee of the enterprise.

LABOR ITEMS 5486719858 - is an integral part of working capital, which is fully consumed in one production cycle; initial inventory (raw materials, materials), which turn into finished products as a result of the impact of tools and with human participation.

LABOR INTENSITY OF THE ANNUAL PROGRAM 648 217519 419 - the total cost of working time necessary to complete the annual production program.

LABOR INTENSITY OF THE PRODUCT 614 512198 718 - the cost of working time on the manufacture of a unit of product or unit of work.

LABOR-INTENSIVE PRODUCTS 719 648519 717 - products whose production is associated with high labor costs.

LABOR-INTENSIVE PRODUCTION 698 191319 81 - is industrial production, where the largest share in the cost estimate comes to wages.

LABOR MECHANIZATION 54871231949 – Leading part of the cost of fixed assets, which is the basis for the assessment of the technical level of production, divided by the average number of workers.

LABOR MARKET 59872151964 - is a set of legal entities that provide employment to the able-bodied population, organize the training and retraining of the temporarily unemployed population and provide its material support.

LABOR MIGRATION 61971549871 - movement of the able-bodied population as a result of changes in the economic situation in places of labor application.

LABOR PERFORMANCE 598 649719 817 - coefficient characterizing by over-fulfillment of normalized time-consuming of operation, of the details or of the product. It is to be defined as the ratio of normalized labor intensity to the actual labor time consuming.

LABOR PRODUCTIVITY 49861721948 - is an indicator of the efficiency of the use of labor resources in material production.

LABOR RESOURCES 61481721954 - is an integral part of the company's driving forces, including the able-bodied population of the country, which has special knowledge, professional training and experience to ensure the production process.

LABOR RESOURCES «intellectual and physical qualities» 584 614819 714 - is an able-bodied part of the state's population at the age of legally established borders, with intellectual and physical qualities, as well as special knowledge and experience for the process of production of material goods and performance of services.

LABOR SAVINGS 498713318516 - release of the number of workers achieved as a result.

LAG 481314819371 - is an economic indicator that characterizes the time interval between two interrelated economic phenomena, such as the beginning and completion of construction of the facility, the allocation of capital investments for construction and commissioning of construction sites.

LAW OF DEMAND 318431318491 – law according to which there is an inverse relationship between demand and price, i.e., under certain economic conditions growth of demand results in price decrease; vice versa decrease of demand leads to growth of prices.

LAW OF MONEY CIRCULATION 648518319417 – Economic law for estimation of quantity of cash means which are necessary for particular economy and which are to provide their goods circulation.

LAW OF PROPORTIONALITY 57980151421941 – Dependence provided most rational correlation among production variables contributing to increased efficacy of production.

LAW OF SUPPLY 578149317491 – The law of supply states that (all other things unchanged) an increase in price results in an increase in quantity supplied.

LAW OF VALUE 519498519641 – Law used when estimating of product cost on the basis of socially needed labor inputs for its production.

LEASE 49718016541 – temporary handover by property owner (lessor) legal right for the earth, premises, buildings, labor equipment and other active elements of fixed production funds to another individual (lessee).

LEASING 514 612518 214 - is a long-term form of rental of machines, equipment and other types of property, providing for periodic payment of its cost.

LEASING CONTRACT 618 491719 217 - is an agreement between the landlord and the lessee, in which they determine the rights and obligations of each of the parties, i.e., the lease period, conditions of preservation, maintenance, operation of machinery and equipment, etc.

LEGAL CAPACITY 4817190 478 - legal capabilities of legal entities and individuals to create and protect property and personal rights and obligations.

LEGAL ENTITY 518 612319 718 - is an organization, enterprise, firm that, in accordance with the current legislation, acts as an independent bearer of rights and obligations and have the main features of a legal entity.

LEGALIZATION OF CRIMINAL INCOME 614814 - actions of criminal groups to organize fictitious confirmation of the legality of the origin of income.

LETTER 319314 898 61 - generalized name of documents of different content that serve as a means of communication between institutions and between institutions and individuals.

LETTER OF CREDIT 519481919 89 – a document containing the order of one credit institution to another to pay the holder of the amount specified therein.

LETTER OF GUARANTEE 21 918 614 - a document confirming the fulfillment of any obligations.

LEND 31848561 - transfer of property for temporary use for a fixed fee.

LEVEL OF TRUST 678 491316 497 - technical and economic assessment of the impact of each indicator included in the relevant group of technical or economic indicators that determine the relative level of competitiveness of production or products.

LIBERALIZATION 614 812498 71 - economic freedom in the market as a consequence of the termination of all restrictions on the economic activity of producers and intermediaries acting in the market.

LICENCE 54856748994 – Permission to use the product of intellectual work within the time allowed for a certain amount of remuneration.

LICENCE AGREEMENT 21487131978 – Official state instrument confirmed right of corporate body or individual to exercise business activity (production, trade, services etc.), financial operations for international business services and use of patented documentary and so on.

LICENCE TRADE 56457281421 - Instrument for trade of technology, certified by patents, licenses of inventions, know-how, commercial know ledges.

LICENCE-HOLDER 286148214278 – Individual or corporate body buying right to use inventions, patents and other technical solutions.

LICENSE TRADING 56457281421 - is a form of trading in technology represented by patents, licenses, know-how, commercial knowledge.

LICENSE 54856748994 - permission to use the product of intellectual labor within the prescribed period for a certain amount of remuneration.

LICENSE AGREEMENT 21487131978 - is an official state document confirming the right of a legal entity or individual to carry out economic activities (production, trade, services, etc.), financial transactions for foreign economic services, use of patented documentation, etc.

LICENSOR 219714854891 - is an individual or legal entity that transfers to the buyer (licensee) for a certain fee its copyright to use the invent, technical or technological solution within the prescribed period.

LICENSEE 286148214278 - is an individual or legal entity that buys the right to use copyright inventions, patents and other technical solutions.

LICENSING 69849871949 - is a type of state regulation of entrepreneurial activity by means of issuing permits (licenses) on certain conditions for the right to carry out activities in the field of production and sell goods and services in order to make a visit.

LICENSOR 219714854891 - is an individual or legal entity that transfers to the buyer (licensee) for a certain fee its copyright to use the invent, technical or technological solution within the prescribed period.

LICENSOR 219714854891 – Individual or corporate body handed over to buyer (licensee) for appropriate fee their copyright for use of invention, technical or technological solution within frames of stated term.

LIFE CYCLE OF INNOVATION 798217298218 - is a period of time from the origin of the idea of creating a future product (technology) or service to the moment of its (its) removal from production.

LIFE CYCLE OF THE ENTERPRISE 819714319612 - eco-economically justified period of economic activity of the enterprise.

LIMIT PRODUCT 64821749879 - is the result of using an additional unit of resource to provide an additional product.

LIMIT YIELD 519 613318 49 - the maximum profit achieved as a result of changes in the output structure by increasing the share of highly profitable products.

LIMITATIVE PRICING 61482 – Strategy of firm prevailed on market provided decrease of market for goods and services close to the level as low as economically reasonable for competitors.

LIMITED 51486417 - liability of legal entities for their obligations, limited by the amount of share capital.

LIMITED LIABILITY 548 612219 71 - liability of the shareholder on the debts of the joint-stock company; may not exceed the value of shares belonging to him.

LIMITED LIABILITY COMPANY 319 617219714 - is an economic company whose founders are responsible for failure to fulfill the obligations assumed by the company within the value of their contributions.

LIMITING PRICING 61482 - is a strategy of the dominant company in the market, providing for lowering the price of goods and services to a level that is not economically justified for competitors.

LIQUID ASSETS 548517219419 – Integrity of cash means and other assets by means of which an owner performs payments for current credit liabilities.

LIQUID ASSETS «transferred to cash» 598671319714 - funds easily transferred to cash; balances in bank current accounts, inventory and other elements of property that can be quickly sold and included in the amount for repayment of debts on obligations.

LIQUID FUNDS 548517219419 - a set of cash and other assets with the help of which their owner makes payments on current and credit obligations.

LIQUIDATION VALUE 498 621314851 - is the cost of selling physically worn fixed assets (usually at the price of scrap metal).

LIQUIDATION OF MAIN PRODUCTION FUNDS 498 712619 714 - write-off of fixed assets from the balance sheet of the enterprise due to physical wear and tear and moral aging, lack of production needs, etc.

LIQUIDATION OF THE ENTERPRISE (FIRM) 61481481247 - termination of the activities of the enterprise (firm) on the basis of a court decision to declare it invalid, in connection with the expiration of the period for which it was established, by the decision of the general meeting (for JSC), a higher body (for state-owned enterprises).

LIQUIDITY 419 498519 717 - the possibility of turning the assets of an enterprise, firm into cash to repay the arrears on obligations.

LIQUIDITY MANAGEMENT 694 712814 914 - is a change of organizational and technical measures aimed at ensuring the timely transformation of their assets into funds for calculation of liabilities.

LIQUIDITY OF THE COMPANY (ENTERPRISE) 516814514817 - the company's ability to repay its obligations in a timely manner.

LIVING OF THE ECONOMY 564317319818 - is a stable economic situation of a state that purposefully pursues its policy under any influence of internal and external socio-economic conditions.

LOGISTICS 714891319481 - is a discipline that studies the processes of management, organization, planning and control of material flows that allow for the promotion of tangible and intangible objects in the field of production process and product sales.

LOAN 31489721851 - type of relationship, contract, under the terms of which one party transfers money or other material values to the other party to the Borrower, and the borrower undertakes to return the same amount of money or material values.

LOAN «payment of interest» 318 648219 714 - transfer by an individual or legal entity of money or property to another individual or legal entity on the terms of return after a certain period, taking into account the payment of interest for the use of the loan.

LOAN PROCEEDS 314964818571 – Part of working capital, supply source of which is to be short term credit.

LOAN TERM 548 647218 917 - is the period of time during which the loanee is obliged to repay the entire loan amount, taking into account the interest rate for the use of the loan.

LOANABLE FUNDS 689721219497 – Monetary capital the owner of which presents a sum of money to disposal of corporate body (enterprise, firm) at a certain payment which is to be a loan interest.

LOCAL MARKET 5196854871- is a market situation in which between producers (sellers) and consumers (buyers) of goods or services develops within a certain territorial zone (city, district, etc.).

LOGISTICS 714891319481 – Discipline that studies the processes of management, organization, planning and control of material flows that allow the promotion of tangible and intangible objects in the field of production and sales.

LONG-TERM LOAN 514819519471 - is a loan issued by a financial and credit institution for the reconstruction and expansion of existing and construction of new enterprises, provided that it is returned within 5 years.

LOSS 714 482519 648 - in the economic practice of enterprises and other individuals and legal entities - loss of inventory and money as a result of the transfer of expenses over income, actual costs of production over planned, current costs of production over proceeds from its sale.

LOSS POINT 498 431485 471 - is an economic situation at the enterprise, in which the proceeds from the sale of products are less than the current production costs.

LOWER LIMIT PRICE 819498219 614 - is the lower limit of the price at which the producer is reimbursed for the current production costs and profit calculated on the basis of the profitability standard is provided.

LUMP SUM PAYMENT 3174984711- is an integral part of the qualification agreement, reflecting the amount of payment for the use of the license. The amount of payment is set as a percentage of the economic effect that the license buyer will receive as a result of its use.

M

MACHINE CAPACITY OF THE ANNUAL PROGRAM 548 497497 17 - time of release of the entire nomenclature and volume of items processed on the machine during the year.

MACHINE CAPACITY OF THE PART 614185498714 - the processing time of the part on the machine in accordance with the technological conditions, which is measured in minutes and hours.

MACHINE UTILIZATION 518671319148 – Indicator of equipment usage within a shift time expressing share of actual time of equipment work over a certain period (shift, day, quarter and so on) within integral operating time fund of installed equipment for appropriate period.

MACHINERY AND EQUIPMENT 518421578491- is a group of basic production assets, including: power machines and equipment that are designed to generate and convert energy; working machines and equipment used directly to influence the object of labor or move it in the process of creating products or providing services, i.e., for direct participation in the technological process.

MACROECONOMICS 719489519617 - is a section of economic science devoted to the study of economic problems and situations at the national economic level, such as changes in national income, investment and tax policy, theoretical aspects of determining the need for labor, methodology for assessing inflation, unemployment, etc.

MAINTENANCE AND REPAIR OF TECHNOLOGICAL EQUIPMENT 648 471819 472 - a set of measures to ensure the operability of the equipment.

MAIN NON-PRODUCTION FUNDS 619 717498 219 - are long-term non-production facilities that retain their natural form and lose their value in parts in the process of their consumption.

MAIN TECHNOLOGICAL EQUIPMENT PARK 49831731881- is a part of the equipment park used to perform technological operations for the production of products.

MAIN PRODUCTION FUNDS 914 917219 716 - are means of labor that repeatedly participate in the production process, performing qualitatively different functions.

MAIN PRODUCTION WORKERS 514 614851318 - a group of workers involved directly in the production process by influencing labor methods by tools.

MANAGEMENT 47854931961 - a set of methods, methods and means of managing a company (enterprise) in market conditions in order to maximize profits.

MANAGER 54931721854 - specialist in the organization and management of production; professional manager endowed with executive power.

MANAGER 54931721854 – Expert in the organization and management of production, professional manager vested with executive power.

MANUFACTURER 497 214318 471 - is an individual or legal entity organizing the production of products.

MANUFACTURER EXPENSES 698518319418 – Manufacturer's expenses included maintenance expenditures for sales department, marketing services, transportation-forwarding operations, other services and so on.

MANUFACTURER STRATEGY 614 897319 648 - is an integral part of the product policy aimed at the production of goods with minimal costs as a result of the use of cheaper material and labor resources, the growth of the image of the enterprise and goods, increasing the level of competitiveness of production and products.

MANUFACTURING APPLICATION OF A PRODUCT 891564319712 – Product life-cycle phase provided production of small product quantity for estimate of the buyers' reaction towards the consumer goods attributes of a product.

MANUFACTURING AUTOMATION 5163187194198 17 – Process of machinery production where technological operations, control and supervision are to be made through the use of machinery, instrumentation and automation devices.

MARKDOWN 574 648319 717 - decrease in the originally set price of the goods.

MARGIN 948518219471 - income received on the difference in percent, which are established for the loan issued by the customer and for attracting funds to the bank.

MARGIN COSTS 489513317485 - gross production costs that are growing or decreasing as a result of changes in unit cost due to a hundred or falling production.

MARGIN EXPENDITURES 489513317485 – Total costs of production that are rising or falling as a result of changes in unit costs due to the rise or fall in output.

MARGINAL INCOME 698 71489851 - income growth as a result of the sale of an additional unit of production.

MARGINAL INCOME «REVENUE» 51482131957 - income (REVENUE) received as a result of the sale of an additional unit of manufactured products.

MARGIN OF PROFIT 614217 – Profit share in the cost of goods sold. It is to be calculated as the ratio of income to sales revenue.

MARGIN PORFIT 51482131957 – Income (proceeds) derived from the sale of an additional unit of output.

MARGINALISM 548518317617 - is a direction in economic science that studies economic situations using limit values, such as marginal costs, minimum wages, marginal interest rate, etc.

MARKUP 69831721941 - artificial price increase to pay for the services of supply organizations; agreed surcharge for the fulfillment by the manufacturer (supplier) of additional requirements of the buyer.

MARKET 59862481979 - is a system of economic relations arising in the field of commodity production as a result of the development and distribution of goods and services during the purchase and sale.

MARKET CAPACITY 548916219718 - estimated value of supply (potential revenue) at a given price level, sales volume for a certain period.

MARKET CONCEPT 519 417 - is a concept according to which the producer should focus on the consumer and market situation, as well as provide for a detailed study of demand, economic behavior and opportunities of buyers.

MARKET CONDITIONS 598642319 718 - is a periodic economic situation characterized by a set of features and reflects the economic condition of the goods market.

MARKET ECONOMY 598 642719 914 - is an economic situation for which the main condition for the development of the country's economy is the laws of commodity production, i.e., demand, supply, laws of value, etc.

MARKET EXIT 598471319718 – market economic circumstances representative for a separate commodity manufacturer, production of which cannot provide an ample income in the course of long period due to low competitive ability.

MARKET FORECASTING 61431781941 - is a scientifically substantiated assumption about the change in market potential: demand, price dynamics, solvency of buyers, level of competitiveness of products, etc.

MARKET FUNCTIONS 618319318516 - a set of functions performed in the process of commodity circulation and satisfaction of demand for inventory and services through interrelated purchase and sale transactions between buyer and seller.

MARKET LIQUIDITY 514 712519 61 - the ability of the market to respond to changes in supply and demand by attracting buyers and sellers.

MARKET PRICE 398 698218 61 - the price at which the purchase and sale of goods in the relevant market takes place.

MARKET SATURATION 498517319641 - market situation when there is no growth in sales of goods.

MARKET SHARE 598713 218064 19 - the share of the goods of the determined producer in the total value of the supply of the relevant goods presented on the market by various suppliers.

MARKET STRUCTURE 714 864914 712 - the main characteristics of the market: the number of producers represented on the market and the volume of their sales; the share of firms with a similar or interchangeable range of goods; quantitative assessment of incoming and outgoing producers from a particular market.

MARKET STRUCTURE NORM 69831721941 - the absence of a dominant role of one commodity producer among widely represented competitors.

MARKET OF GOODS AND SERVICES 48949719857 - is an analytical section of the business plan, which allows, on the basis of the results of analyzing the capabilities of existing markets, demand for products (services) of the firm, to determine the market segments accepted for the company's products, predetermine possible niches, assess the potential capacity of markets, planned and actual.

MARKET NICHE 948512 61971 18 - is a part of the market (segment) not mastered by entrepreneurs.

MARKET SECTOR 31489481951 - is an enlarged part of the market in which the product policy of the enterprise is formed under the influence of tastes and needs of buyers.

MARKET SEGMENT 548 647194 821 - is part of the market of goods whose main consumers are united by common interests.

MARKET SEGMENTATION 518 613910 648 - division of the market into segments on certain grounds, for example, by category of buyers, type of product, etc.

MARKET PARADIGM 198682718014 - is a set of concepts and principles that reveal the effectiveness of market processes.

MARKET PRIORITIES 519 674 819 6 - advantages in the process of meeting the specific needs of the buyer.

MARKETING 619481578491- is a management system for the field of activity of the company (enterprise) that ensures the movement of goods to the market to meet demand, taking into account the requirements of the buyer and his solvency.

MARKETING COMPETITION 548 614219 718 – Development of conditions (planning) provided enterprise's business aims' achievement towards satisfying of separate markets' demand with more competitive goods in comparison with goods of acting competitors.

MARKETING INTERMEDIARIES 64859172861 - legal entities and individuals involved in the sale of finished products and services of an industrial enterprise and goods produced by other enterprises.

MARKETING MANAGEMENT COMPLEXITY 694218719481 – Comprehensive accounting in the course of marketing control of production parameters, sales and consumption.

MARKETING OPPORTUNITY OF THE ENTERPRISE 514212519718 - development and implementation of an action plan to achieve a competitive advantage in the process of production and sale of products.

MARKETING PLAN 689710192 4 - is a section of the business plan that reflects specific strategies for setting prices and sales of finished products, methods of stimulating re-clining activities, market concept of company management.

MARKETING PRINCIPLE 51431881947 - in accordance with marketing theory, the basic principles of this management system are aimed at ensuring the growth of the level of profitability of production and products, improving production and marketing activities in accordance with market interests, positioning, analyzing the state of existing markets and prognosing the prospects for its development, etc.

MARKETING PRINCIPLE 51431881947 - in accordance with marketing theory, the basic principles of this management system are aimed at ensuring the growth of the level of profitability of production and products, improving production and marketing activities in accordance with market interests, positioning, analyzing the state of existing markets and prognosing the prospects for its development, etc.

MARKETING SERVICE 498 197519 814 - a set of subdividing of the enterprise engaged in planning sales volume, analyzing existing markets in terms of demand, price, capabilities of competitors, etc.

MASS PRODUCTION 64914871961 - is a progressive form of production organization that provides significant volumes of output of related products with a high concentration of economical and productive equipment and the expansion of subject specialization.

MATERIAL AND TECHNICAL RESOURCES 56417492 - a set of labor items (raw materials, materials, fuel, etc.) and tools (machines and equipment) processing labor items.

MATERIAL CONSUMPTION OF PRODUCT498471 – Economic indicator of the value of material costs that is fitted to1monetary unit either of product prime cost, or of the gross production cost.

MATERIAL COSTS 81947148851 - a set of items or cost elements involved in the formation of a unit cost or production cost estimate.

MATERIAL FLOWS 61971841 - a set of material values (raw materials, materials, parts, semi-finished products, components) that move over time along the technological route for consistent execution Operations (procurement, machining, assembly operations) related to the manufacture of finished products, as well as warehousing and transportation of manufactured products to the consumer.

MATERIAL INCENTIVE 104218314261 - material goods to stimulate work.

MATERIAL INTENSITY OF PRODUCTS 498471 - is an economic indicator reflecting the cost of material costs per one «1» monetary unit of production cost or the cost of gross output.

MATERIAL MOVEMENTS 61971841 – aggregate of material values (raw materials, components, semi-finished products, components), which move in time of technological route for consistent operations (procurement, machining and assembly operations) related to the manufacture of finished products, as well as storage and transportation of goods manufactured to consumer.

MATERIAL RESOURCES 549317219614 - means of production, i.e., tools and labor items created to ensure the process of material production: machines, equipment, tools, devices, raw materials, materials, semi-factories, etc.

MATERIAL RESOURCE CONSUMPTION RATE 61857141989 - the maximum permissible rate of consumption of raw materials, fuel, energy per unit of production. There are annual, operational-technical, single, consolidated norms.

MATERIALS UTILIZATION RATE 689 712498 47 – rational utilization of material resources (raw materials), which is a ratio of the weight of the finished product to the total material utilization per unit of production or per work piece weight.

MARRIAGE 618471318684 - establishment of the official commission of the proportion of marriage as a result of detected deviations from approved standards or specifications.

MEANS OF LABOR 549 498317 318 - a set of material means by which the worker affects the premiums labor, changing their physical and chemical properties.

MEANS OF PRODUCTION 694 718519 642 - a set of means and objects of labor used in the process of material production (machines, equipment, raw materials, materials, etc.).

MESOECONOMICS 58947569418 - is a scientific discipline that studies economic processes at the level of sectors of the national economy and large associations.

MECHANICAL EQUIPMENT OF LABOR 54871231949 - is the cost of the leading part of fixed assets, which serves as the basis for assessing the technical level of production, classified as the average number of employees.

MICROECONOMICS 69831721841- is a scientific discipline that studies relatively small-scale economic interests and objects (enterprises, firms).

MICROENVIRONMENT 514819519716 - is a set of socio-economic principles of the enterprise that ensure its effective functioning in the market.

MINERALS 219 815317 64 - natural vents of both organic and inorganic origin (e.g., oil, gas, precious stones, ore, etc.), which are used in the field of production as materials, materials, energy resources.

MINERAL SUPPLY 619 714819 917 - Numerical estimate of mineral formation of earth crust (supply of coal, oil, gas and so on) made as a result of geological research.

MIXED ECONOMY 517219319648 - is an economy characterized by the presence of various forms of ownership.

MODERNIZATION OF EQUIPMENT 548164918 - improvement, renewal of equipment, machines, technological processes in order to increase labor productivity and improve their economic indicators.

MONETARY AND CREDIT POLICY 519318619712 - Set of organization financial measures and methods focused on economic development regulation, deterrence of monetary means depreciation and provision of payment balance equilibrium.

MONETARY CAPITAL 47182849951 - One of functional form of industrial capital utilized at the stages of start and conclusion of its circulation; monetary means located in banking account of enterprise.

MONEY SUPPLY 564318518712 - funds in circulation.

MONETARY POLICY 519318619712 - is a set of organizational and financial measures and methods aimed at regulating economic development, containing depreciation of funds and ensuring equal balance of payments.

MONETARY POLICY 519318619712 - is a set of organizational and financial measures and methods aimed at regulating economic development, containing depreciation of funds and ensuring equal balance of payments.

MONITORING 21046101968 - a constant study of the economic activities of enterprises, organizations and other economic facilities.

MONOPOLY 348612317514 - is the exclusive right of individuals, legal entities or the state to form a commodity policy, regulate prices and sales of goods.

MONOPOLY COMPETITION MARKET 59879481978 - is a type of competition when the entire product range is represented on the market by a large number of producers, whose products are not only specialized, but also differentiated.

MONOPOLY PRICE 614891391718 - is the market price for goods and services, which is set above or below the cost of goods (services) depending on the interests of commodity drivers who occupy a monopoly position in the market.

MONOPSONIA 91851631947 - is an economic situation in the market in which a large number of competing sellers serve one monopolist buyer.

MORAL RISK 61214954718 - is the behavior of a legal entity or individual aimed at consciously increasing the risk of loss. At the same time, they are supposed to be covered at the expense of the insurance company.

MORATORIUM 61821331941 - postponement of obligations to repay the loan, perform operations on debt approvals.

MORTGAGE 698712319714 – Pledge of real property aimed at getting of long term (10-20 years) monetary loan. Paying of a loan includes rate of interest on credit.

MORTGAGE BANK 64848171842 – Loan institution established for long term crediting against security of immovable property (land, city buildings etc.) with restriction in the right of disposal.

MORTGAGE MARKET 564814 – Variety of loan markets in which mortgage bonds issued against security of immovable property work out as a subject of sales-purchasing.

MOTIVATION 498714 - is a condition for the effective implementation of the decision on the basis of material or moral stimulation of any activity. Negative motivation is manifested in the imposition of sanctions (repression, reduction of the premium percentage, etc.).

MOTIVATIONAL ANALYSIS 648317219 - is a direction of marketing research related to identifying the causes of changes in consumer behavior in the market and assessing their impact on changes in demand.

MOTIVATIONAL RESEARCH 648317219 – Area of focus of market research related to the identification of the causes of changes in consumer behavior in the market; and to an assessment of their impact on the change in demand.

MULTI-STAND SERVICE 5485491941 - work of one machine worker on two or more machines. Helps to reduce equipment downtime and increase productivity.

MUTUAL EXCLUDING ALTERNATES 564891319718 - Project variants provided the same aim implementation. Most effective variant is admitted for fulfillment.

N

NATIONAL DEBT 584891619471 - Total sum of government's liability includes outstanding loan sum and debt unpaid interest.

NATIONAL INCOME 564718319741 - Indicator of economic development of the country which expresses modified form of surplus value (revenue) plus commission for rendering of services in non-productive sphere.

NATIONALIZATION 31981251914 - the decision of the state to seize or redeem private enterprises, organizations or property with subsequent transfer to state ownership.

NET DISCOUNTED INCOME 514216519718 - is an economic indicator used to choose the most effective option for an investment project.

NET DISTRUBUTION COST 518 718319 217 - Expenses connected to sales-purchasing of the goods.

NET PRODUCTS 819714319612 - is an economic asset defined as the difference between gross output and the amount of material costs and depreciation; in other words, it is wages plus profit.

NET PROFIT 516318319717 - profit left at the disposal of the enterprise after taxes. Calculated as the difference between gross profit and payments to the budget.

NEW COST 49861271941 - this type of cost consists of two parts. The first is the cost of labor production, reflecting the socially necessary working time, i.e., the part of the worker's time that is spent on the reproduction of the equivalent of the cost of labor and is estimated by the wages of the worker. The other, most part, i.e., surplus time, is the source of creating surplus value, which is fully appropriated by the producer.

NEW FIXED CAPITAL FORMATION 564181798164 – planned commissioning of reconstructed and extended capital construction objects.

"NICHE" IN CONSUMER DEMAND 31971236149 - availability of a nomenclature of goods that do not meet the requirements of buyers. As a result, there is a deficit and it is possible to enter the market with products that meet the scarce needs of the buyer.

NOMINAL WAGE 614 812319 71 – Monetary terms of payment for labor according to effectiveness of labor.

NON-DIRECT EXPENSES 316 718549 612 – Current expenses which may be referred to appropriate article finishing because they are connected to operation of workshop or enterprise in the whole for instance expenses on running and maintenance of equipment, workshop expenses.

NON-ELASTIC DEMAND 564814319583 - is a market situation in which the proceeds from the sale of an increased volume of goods do not cover the losses from the decrease in its price.

NON-PRODUCTION COSTS 719 314 5198042178 - current costs not directly related to the implementation of the production process.

NON-PRODUCTIVE EXPEDNDITURE 498612719714 - Included in full cost total current expenditures not connected directly to product manufacturing process.

NON-PRICE COMPETITION 598571 - reflection of the quality and novelty of the goods, the level of service and the progress of forms of implementation, taking into account the specific interests of buyers, etc.

NORM 5713196194 - sample, measure, maximum allow consumption or size, established measure.

NORM «indicator» 48951721981 - is a technical and economic indicator reflecting the limit value of the parameter, the level of use of the resource.

NORM FOR MARKET STRUCTURE 69831721941 - Absence of dominant role of one producer among well represented competitors.

NORM OF CONDUCT IN THE MARKET 69831729851 - lack of collusion between producers represented on the market and forced methods of competition. There is an ever-growing demand for a wide range of products.

NORM OF WORKING CAPITAL IN UNFINISHED PRODUCTION 56482131981 - the cost of products at different stages of the production process: from start-up to production to the production of finished products.

NUMBER OF EMPLOYEES AT THE ENTERPRISE 61971381948 - is an indicator reflecting the average number of industrial, production and non-industrial personnel.

NUMBER OF INDUSTRIAL - PRODUCTION PERSONNEL 498319489818 - includes categories of workers involved in production: workers, engineering and technical workers, junior service personnel, etc.

NUMBER OF MAIN WORKERS 518 485319 47 - is determined depending on the labor intensity of divisions, the annual volume of production of products, the annual fund of working hours of one worker.

NUMBER OF NON-INDUSTRIAL PERSONNEL 319 718219 814 - includes categories of workers engaged in the non-industrial sphere of the enterprise, i.e. workers supporting buildings, structures in working condition; staff of medical and children's institutions, etc.

O

OBJECT OF INVESTMENT ACTIVITY 619718 510691 - use of funds for replenishment Fixed and working capital, securities, intellectual labor products, etc.

OBJECT-WISE ANALYSIS OF CONTINUOUS MARKETS 514819319617 – provides appropriate types of works for the following objects of research: the scope of the circulation of commodities -the procedure of purchase and sale for a profit; the product of labor, created for exchange and sales; legal or natural persons who consume goods of production; competition.

OFFER 51457149847 - is an official offer to conclude a purchase and sale transaction between individuals or legal entities.

OFFER «contractual price» 516489488 - nomenclature of products presented on the market of goods by the seller (manufacturer of goods or his representative) for sale at a set or contractual price.

OFFER CURVE 489 471819 498 - is a curve that graphically reflects the law of supply, according to which when the price increases, the supply increases.

OFFER FUNCTION 514518914217 - mathematical dependence of the cost of the volume of manufactured inventory and services offered entering the relevant markets (the amount of supply) on such factors as the cost of resources, efficiency of technological processes, tax policy, competitiveness, prices for similar goods and services, etc.

OFFER TABLE 489 748987 615 - is a summary table reflecting the volume of offers of a certain product at different prices for it.

OFFER VALUE 689714219817 - valuation of the quantity of certain goods provided for sale at a set price within a given period of time.

OFFER VOLUME 808491 47 - the quantity of certain goods that the manufacturer or supplier offers for sale on the market.

OFFERENT 498641 074981 - a physical or legal person making an offer.

OLIGARCHY 498 715319 718 - is a form of government by a group of independent and influential people belonging to the political, economic, industrial elite.

OLIGOPOLIA 519 712614 178 - dominance in the production and market of a certain goods of a small number of commodity drivers.

OLIGOPSONY 489 47149818 - is a market situation characterized by the presence of monopoly groups of buyers of a certain product that have a great impact on the set of market prices, changes in the volume of purchases.

OLIGOPOLISTIC MARKET 56421971981 - is a market that occupies a large space, but the pace of its development is limited, on the one hand, by the net monopoly market, and on the other hand, by the monopolistic competition market.

OPERATING COEFFICIENTS 589 712619 74 - indicators of the company's activities, reflecting the ratio of profit and costs, i.e., profit per monetary unit of expenditure.

OPERATIONAL LEVEL OF MANAGEMENT MARKET 917 614219 61 - feasibility study of the tasks to be solved, implemented according to the plan of the general strategy of the enterprise.

OPERATION RESEARCH 584214 – development and use of various methods of applied mathematics to optimize solutions to socio-economic and production-economic problems.

OPERATIONAL MANAGEMENT 898 916517 - development of management decisions to ensure the timely execution of planned work based on the use of operational and calendar plans and shift tasks in the basis of each production unit, site, workplace.

OPERATIONAL LEVEL OF MANAGEMENT MARKET 917 614219 61 - feasibility study of the tasks to be solved, implemented according to the plan of the general strategy of the enterprise.

OPPORTUNITIES OF THE COMPANY 598782614016 - is a section of the business plan that reflects the main directions of the company's production activities with an indication of goals (volume of production and implementation, ensuring revenue and profit, increasing the share of the company's products (services) in the markets) and the plan of organizational and technical measures for their implementation.

ORDER 316714518971 - agreement, contract executed between manufacturer (seller) and buyer where consumer interest in purchasing (buy) of certain goods with notification of all necessary technical and economic features (price, quantity, quality) and delivery terms including responsibility for goods safety is expressing.

ORDER PORTFOLIO 819 714319 617 - a set of orders held by the company (enterprise); a condition for the formation of the production program of the enterprise, which allows you to determine the real load of production capacity to fulfill orders in accordance with the requirements of the customer.

ORGANIZATION OF PRODUCTION 498 617 - is the process of rational unification of labor resources with material elements of production to ensure the planned production of finished products and the performance of services, taking into account the minimization of costs and labor intensity of products.

ORIGINAL DOCUMENT 598 641317064819 - original copy of the document.

OTHER PRODUCTION COSTS 318471216814 - expenses that are determined on the basis of special calculations and, as a rule, are included in the cost of the relevant products.

OVERHEAD COSTS 614819319718 – is an integral part of self-cost, reflecting the additional costs of organization, management, technical preparation of production, etc.

OVERHEADS 51948148 – Part of the cost, which reflects the additional costs for the organization, management, technical preparation of production, etc.

OVERPRODUCTION 51961231961 - is an economic situation in which the volume of goods (offer) or services produced exceeds the real need (demand) and the goods can be sold only at reduced, even unprofitable targets.

OVERPRODUCTION CRISIS 4851481619 71- is a situation in which manufactured goods are not sold due to exceeding real need.

OVERTIME 498714918217 - work in excess of the working hours established by law.

OWN WORKING CAPITAL 519 648319 712 - part of working capital that characterizes property independence and financial stability of the enterprise.

OWNER 549317 498174 - is a natural or legal person who has the rights to own, use and dispose of property.

OWNERSHIP LAW 561481 - consolidation of legal norms for the protection of material goods of individuals and legal entities in accordance with the legislation of the Russian Federation.

P

PAPERWORK MANAGEMENT 516489498517 - fulfilled by office and management personnel operations connected to papers (documentation) processing.

PAYBACK 719 648219 71 - is the period during which expenses are reimbursed by income received from the activities of the enterprise.

PASSIVE DEMAND GOODS 598 641219 718 - goods presented on the market, but not in demand by buyers, i.e., belonging to a narrow market segment, for example, foreign and fashionable goods, precious metal products, etc.

PAST WORK 518549719612 - labor embodied in the means of production (machines, equipment, raw materials, materials, etc.). Unlike live labor, it does not create new value, but is a condition for its creation.

PARADOX OF VALUE 748549 - high consumer value of goods at low exchange value (price).

PASSIV 619714 - is the right side of the balance sheet, reflecting the sources of formation of the enterprise's funds, its funding, grouped by their ownership and recognition.

PASSIVE PART OF THE MAIN PRODUCTION FUNDS 89482149561 - is an auxiliary part of fixed production assets (buildings, structures, etc.) that ensure the process of operation of active elements.

PATENT 498792514 - is a document certifying the author's right to the invention, as well as permission to use the invention. The latter is valid for a certain period of time established by law.

PATENT HOLDER 5186173194 - is a natural or legal person who has the exclusive right of the author to use the invention at his own discretion.

PENALTIES 498517219491 - payments paid by one of the parties for violation of obligations fixed in the agreement in order to compensate for damages.

PENALTY 69831757489 – the amount of the fine for violation or poor-quality performance by one of the parties of the terms of the agreement.

PENALTY 684397 - is a type of penalty, fine for violation by an individual or legal entity of the obligations of the agreement. Accrued for each day of late payment as a percentage of the amount of late payments or outstanding duties.

PENSION 219471 - is a form of gentle support for citizens who have reached retirement age established by law.

PERFORMANCE 319418514814 – cost of a product manufactured over a certain period, related to one working on or laboring man from industrial personnel.

PERFORMANCE RATE 69874149817 – fixed amount of work, designed for one or a group of employees, to be executed over a period of time (hour, day, etc.) along with consistency of labor conditions.

PETRODOLLARS 5648141 – state revenues from the export of oil and other energy resources.

PERSONNEL OF INDUSTRIAL ENTERPRISE 4813164 - quantitative and functional characteristics of the personnel of an industrial enterprise directly or indirectly involved in the manufacture of finished products, organization and management of production.

PHYSISCAL DEPRECIATION 54861271949 – Process of fixed capital elements' physical aging because of which the elements become useless for further utilization at production site.

PIECE-CALCULATION TIME NORM 519418313184 - norm of time required for production Units of production, and preparatory and final time.

PHASES OF THE ECONOMIC CYCLE 619314 801316846 - cycle of stages, i.e., peak, recession or crisis, depression, recovery, recovery.

PHYSICAL WEAR COEFFICIENT OF EQUIPMENT 53012450818 - is an indicator reflecting the share of the initial cost of equipment transferred to finished products.

PLACEMENT OF PRODUCTION 81972489471 - territorial and economic distribution of material production, taking into account the availability of sources of raw materials and able-bodied population of the region.

PLAN 21971231481 - is a system of activities or tasks united by a common goal, which provides for their implementation on time and in a certain sequence.

PLANNING 471 814821 4 - is a management function that is involved in making decisions on the main directions of economic development of the company, enterprise based on the development of quantitative and qualitative indicators, as well as in the identification of ways to implement them.

PLANNING HORIZON 518516319719 819 – period of plan validity (quarter, year and five years).

PLEDGE 519016 914571 – Property and other material values which are construed as securing of the credit.

POINT OF INDIFFERENCE 489 497513 497 - is the economic condition in the activities of the enterprise, when the current costs of additional production are equal to the revenue received from the sale of these products.

POLYPOLIA 514 712319 714 - is a market situation in which the number of large producers is limited.

POPULATION EMPLOYMENT 218 494517601 – Socio-economic description that expresses formation, distribution and use of labor force on the basis of the estimate of people's opportunities and working activity, availability of appropriate education and established salary.

POWER MEASUREMENT UNIT 319617319489 - is a planned unit of measurement of the number of machines, equipment, devices, engine power installed on tires and equipment for their driving, performance (labor intensity, machine capacity, production).

POSITION 317421898516 – a certain position to be taken up by a person who is accomplishing organizational, administering and commercial duties at the system of an enterprise management.

POVERTY THRESHOLD 491 216498 27 - is an officially established minimum income limit below which recipients of this income belong to the poor population.

PREFERENTIAL LOAN 618 471219 714 - a loan received on preferential terms, i.e., with a lower interest rate and a longer maturity of the loan received.

PREFERENTIAL PROFIT 61971251949 - is part of gross income that is not partially or completely taxed in accordance with the current legislation.

PRELIMINARY EXAMINATION OF INVESTMENT PROJECT 619 71481 - justification of expediency and Viability of the project, taking into account the interests of the customer (borrower) and creditor (investor), as well as the complexity of the project, risk penalties, the volume of capital investments and the share of their advance by year of development and implementation of the project.

PRE-PRODUCTION STAGE 61971281914 - is a stage of the product life cycle, at which research work is carried out to create new competitive products, design documentation is developed and the sequence of technological operations, the need for technological equipment, etc. is established.

PRICE 519491 498 614 718712 - monetary expression of the value of goods; an economic category that allows you to indirectly measure the working time spent on the production of goods.

PRICE ADDITIVE 6983172194 - markup to the price list price for goods and services for the urgency of delivery or performance of services, higher quality of goods.

PRICES COMPARABLE 318 648219 717 - prices given by value to the conditions of a certain period for a certain date.

PRICE COMPETITION 519 618319 714 - rivalry between producers based on lower prices for similar goods.

PRICE CONTROL 498 471213 485 - a set of state measures to regulate wholesale and retail prices by establishing limit coefficients for their growth. An amount exceeding the upper price limit is withdrawn to the state budget.

PRICE DISCOUNT 319 818916 713 - price reduction as a result of changes in the market situation or the terms of the trade agreement, for example, price discount on seasonal goods.

PRICE FREE 314 713898 64 - is a type of market or contractual price that is set by the producer on the basis of demand or contract between the buyer and the seller.

PRICE FOR INTELLECTUAL PRODUCTS 8 491 798 6 491 - price set on the basis of the balance of economic interests of the producer and consumer, which take into account all technical data, economic characteristics that determine supply and demand.

PRICE INVOICE 914 481219 61 - the price reflected in the document for the delivered goods.

PRICE REDUCTION RATE 51841 - is an indicator used to calculate the price elasticity coefficient, which is defined as the ratio of the old price to the new one.

PRICE REGULATION 59831489947 - is a state procedure for containing the rise in prices for scarce consumer goods of mass demand as a result of replacing state prices with free ones.

PRICE INSENSIBILITY 489317918614 – Market situation in which the price remains the same in case of shortage or surplus goods on the market.

PRICE LIDERSHIP 496 712814 718 – the position of the commodity producer regulating the pricing policy in the market.

PRICE NON-ELASTICITY 489317918614 - is a market situation in which the price remains unchanged in the event of a shortage or surplus of goods in the market.

PRICE PREMIUM 6983172194 – Premium to the list price of goods and services for express delivery or performance of services, a product of higher quality.

PRICES LIMIT 548714821491 – the maximum allowable deviations (growth or fall) for the period of one exchange session.

PRICING 548 621598 317 - the process of pricing for goods and services.

PRINCIPAL CAPITAL 514 719 - is part of the production capital; it is characteristic of the conditions of private property.

PRIVATIZATION 69851671848 - is a type of decentralization of production carried out by transferring or selling property from state ownership to private property.

PRIVATE PROPERTY 519 618317 481 - the right of legal entities and individuals to dispose of their own movement and real estate.

PROCUREMENT LOGISTICS 69871231941 – Subsystem of production management which expresses process performed to meet production need for raw material and other materials. It provides economic estimate for movement of all integrity of material flows along with minimization of expenditures in the course of purchasing, transportation and storage of materials.

PRODUCT 489 643198 494 - is an economic category, a product of labor produced to meet social needs through exchange or sale.

PRODUCT COMPETITIVENESS INDEX 564812319718 - is an indicator of a market economy that reflects the dynamics of changes in consumer properties of goods as a result of various organizational and technical measures and the impact of economic factors.

Product (goods) BY-PRODUCT 519 614 - is a product (goods) that is created simultaneously in the process of manufacturing the main product.

PRODUCT FUND CAPACITY 319718317498 - indicator, reverse fund return; used to determine the needs for fixed assets. It is calculated as the ratio of the average annual value of fixed assets to the value of manufactured products for a certain period.

PRODUCT IDENTIFICATION 564 718574181 - A comparison of actual engineering-and-economical characteristics of goods and the parameters fixed in documentation.

PRODUCT LIABILITY 298712314 - is one of the product quality indicators that characterizes the uptime of the product under specified operating conditions.

PRODUCT LIFE CYCLE 498218514612 - the period from the introduction of goods to the market to the withdrawal of the product from production.

PRODUCT MATURITY 319498 719 618 - stage of life cycle of the article when volume of production is stable.

PRODUCT NOMENCLATURE 2193174194 - a list of goods (services) presented on the market or included in the production plan of the enterprise (firm).

PRODUCT OFFER 589 712498 714 - a set of goods and services presented on the market. The correspondence between supply and demand characterizes the market as balanced.

PRODUCT POSITIONING 618 714217 - is a set of measures to achieve a competitive position of a new product in the market and create conditions for its sale.

PRODUCT POLICY OF THE ENTERPRISE 698 471319 64 - is an integral part of the long-term production development plan (business plan), including a preliminary selection of nomenclate tours of products and services, which should be included in the production portfolio in the future.

PRODUCT RANGE 418 016078498 - a list of products prepared for sale.

PRODUCTION 619 717481 - is the most effective form of production organization, providing for the consistency of technological operations over time, the rhythm of each specialized workplace.

PRODUCTION « technological operations » 51421914 - is a set of interrelated technological operations, in the process of which, with the help of labor and labor, raw materials and material resources are processed and turned into finished products.

PRODUCTION AREA 914818 - is part of the total area of the enterprise, where the entire set of technological operations for the manufacture of finished products and the provision of services is carried out.

PRODUCTION AUTOMATION 516318719419817 - is a process of machine production in which technological operations, control and control are carried out with the help of machines, machinery, devices and automatic devices.

PRODUCTION CAPACITY OF THE ENTERPRISE 514812518491 - the maximum possible volume of production for a certain period (usually for a year, month) with full use of the main production equipment and areas at the enterprise.

PRODUCTION CAPITAL 59871489851 - a set of fixed assets (fixed capital) and working capital (current capital).

PRODUCTION COMMUNICATIONS 497 694319 81 - established production relations between legal entities in the process of production, distribution and consumption of aggregate products of material production (supply of means of production, provision of services, etc.).

PRODUCTION CYCLE 2196148197 - is a stage of the product life cycle, reflecting the period from the beginning of the product production process to its completion.

PRODUCTION CONCENTRATION 548 671319 714 - Manufacturing organization method provided concentration of separate manufacturers' means of production at large-scale enterprises.

PRODUCTION CONTENTS 578491698917 – Numerical evaluation of parts and units' output for the production purposes, divisible by its quantity in unit of each article from number of articles, taking into account a backlog.

PRODUCTION COOPERATION 589 648751 491 - Model of productive connections among specialized enterprises, firms which presented for implementation of cooperative economic activity with usage of allowable deductions (rental, currency, visa, taxation, customs, laborious and so on) provided benevolent conditions for attraction of long term foreign and domestic capital investments.

PRODUCTION DEFECT 54831749816 - parts, assemblies, finished products that do not meet the technical conditions of production and operation.

PRODUCTION DIFFERENTIATION 519414319417 – Design and technological procedure provided change of technical and economic indicators of product which compares favorably with manufactured by enterprise-competitors analogues.

PRODUCTION EXPANSION 64121489871 - new construction, expansion and reconstruction of existing workshops and other production facilities, carried out according to the approved project, taking into account cost estimates.

PRODUCTION FLOW 216 491 - is the maximum volume of production that can be provided by cash and labor.

PRODUCTION INTENSIFICATION 564819319712 – Area of focus aimed at enhanced production efficacy, connected to production volume increase, more effective utilization of material, labor and financial resources on the basis of scientific advance.

PRODUCTION LEAD TIME 914815 419718 – Technological process of a product manufacturing which may be estimated by measure of time from the beginning of first operation to completion of the final technological operation.

PRODUCTION LOGISTICS 619712319418 - movement of economically justified material flows in the process of creating finished products, provided that the supply of raw materials, materials, semi-finished products, intersectoral and general engineering parts for each workplace throughout the entire chain of the technological process is timely and complete.

PRODUCTION LOSSES 61489514 - losses resulting from deviations in the organization of production leading to the irrational use of means of production, such as over-planned downtime of equipment, have increased Material costs for the production of a unit of production, etc.

PRODUCTION STANDARD 69874149817 - the established amount of work calculated for one or a group of employees, which must be performed in a certain period of time (hour, day, etc.) with the agreed working conditions.

PRODUCTION TECHNOLOGY 718 649316 217 - the process of implementing technological operations for processing material resources and turning them into parts with subsequent assembly into a product.

PRODUCTION PERSONNEL 61851731947 - is a part of the able-bodied population that is part of an industrial enterprise and ensures the performance of all functions related to the production process, from the planning of production stocks of material assets, participation in the main and auxiliary technological operations of the production process, services and management of economic activities and up to the sale of finished products.

PRODUCTION PLAN 728 641 49848 - is a section of the business plan that is developed at enterprises related to the field of material production.

PRODUCTION QUALITY 578421316214 – Technical and economic category expressing aggregation of different product (article) properties stipulated capability for satisfying of different public demands.

PRODUCTION RESERVE 49131851864 - stock of commodity and material values, funds, which is created to ensure the continuity of production Process, increasing production, increasing its effectiveness.

PRODUCTION STORE 178 478364714 – material values (raw materials, materials, purchased components, half-finished parts, fuel) and other elements of working capital that are located at enterprise storage; not yet being used in the technological processing.

PRODUCTIVITY IMPROVEMENT PROGRAM 48971231749 - is a set of organizational and technical measures economically based on resources, participants and deadlines, which allows to ensure planned productivity growth at the enterprise.

PROFESSION 214618319 917 - is the main kind, type of activity of the economically active population with certain knowledge, professional suitability (for example, writer, doctor, scientist, teacher, etc.).

PROFIT 61931851971 - is the main goal of entrepreneurial activity; in the conditions of market relations - a transformed form of added value.

PROFIT AND LOSS REPORT 712 617 - report on the results of the enterprise's activities for the year, reflecting information on total revenue from the sale of products and services, profit received and losses incurred.

PROFIT DISTRIBUTION 798641979516 - determination of the share of net profit (dividend) for each founder, as well as for the formation of various funds, reserves, etc.

PROFIT TAXABLE 31851431961 - gross or balance profit reduced by the amount of preferential profit.

PROFITABILITY 498712318491 - profitability, profitability of the enterprise; indicator of economic efficiency of production, reflecting the results of activities.

PROFIT TAX 491819317481 – Is an integral part of retained earnings, which is the source of the redistribution of national income.

PROFIT RATIO 614217 - share of profit in the value of products sold. It is calculated by the attitude of income to sales revenue.

PROFITABILITY COEFFICIENTS 498 614891 471 - coefficients determined by the ratio of profit to cost bridges used in diagnosing the financial condition of the recipient enterprise.

PROFITABILITY RATIOS 498 614891 471 – Coefficients determined by the ratio of profit to the cost used in the diagnosis of the financial condition of the recipient company.

PROGRESSIVE TAXATION 59864131971 – Taxation, providing higher tax rates to the extent of the growth of the total income of the payer.

PROMOTION OF GOODS ON THE MARKET 61431851971 - is a set of organizational and economic measures aimed at increasing demand and increasing sales of goods.

PROPERTY 189 472194898 - ownership of means and products of production to certain persons - individuals or legal entities.

PROPERTY DAMAGE 518319314317 - natural or monetary losses and losses arising as a result of violations in the organization of production, non-fulfillment of contractual conditions, non-compliance of the quality of supplies of material assets with technical specifications or standards.

PROPERTY OF AN ENTERPRISE 218317 489317 – Basic and working capital and also other material values, cost of which is set in independent balance sheet of enterprise, firm.

PROPERTY INSURANCE 519 614812 - is a type of insurance, the object of which is the property of citizens and companies.

PROPERTY SHARE 613 482819718 - property owned by several individuals or legal entities with a certain share for each participant.

PROPERTY STRUCTURE 104 198 498471 - a structure reflecting the share of each element included in the list of property, i.e., the share of fixed assets and non-current assets, mobile assets, stocks and costs, debt, cash and securities.

PROPORTIONAL TAXATION 61931851971 – Taxation, providing a unified tax rate regardless of the total income of the physical or legal person.

PROTECTIONISM 519619498714 - is a state policy aimed at restricting imports by introducing higher tariffs to maintain the competitiveness of domestic goods.

PROVISION OF THE INDUSTRIAL ENTERPRISE WITH MATERIAL RESOURCES 21649829871 - is a period of uninterrupted operation of an industrial enterprise with the appropriate level of use of available inventories.

PUBLIC EMPLOYMENT SERVICE 518728398641 – State institution the purpose of which is providing of public able for work with possibility to take part in occupation aimed at material values' completion through the use of labor instruments as well as to work at non-productive sphere.

PUBLIC ETERPRISE 791849319611 – Productive unit with public liability.

PUNUTIVE AGREEMENT 498217319421 – Officially executed legal agreement among large-scale manufacturers of similar product which provides mutual market research, price regulation, establishment of discounts and etc.

PURCHASED PRODUCTS AND SEMI-FINISHED PRODUCTS 614 715598 17 - is a cost element that includes the cost of purchased products and semi-finished products used in the production of products at one enterprise and services of co-pated enterprises.

PURE COMPETITION 519618319417 - is a market situation with a large number of producers and consumers in equal economic conditions.

PURE MONOPOLY 318614219718 - is a market situation in which the goods are represented by the only producer in the absence of competitors and the presence of various benefits and privileges from the state.

Q

QUALITY CONTROL 598 712894 716 - assessment of compliance of the actual performance characteristics of the product, determining its suitability for consumption, characteristics, approved specifications, standards or customer requirements.

QUALIFICATION 619314894217 - Special training level for personal of enterprise towards fulfillment of a certain type of works and services.

QUALITY PER DESCRIPTION 598319498712 - It is to be based on comparison of goods with description of all technique economic properties noted in the agreement.

QUALITY PER SAMPLE 219518619472 - Evaluation of delivered goods correspondence to representative sample chosen according to stated production specifications.

QUANTITY DEMENDED 31721851427 - cost estimate of certain goods quantity which may be acquired by buyer at established price over a set period of time.

QUANTITY SUPPLIED 689714219817 - cost estimate of certain goods quantity presented for sale at established price over a set period of time.

QUICK ASSETS 598671319714 - Means easy sold for monetary means; residuals at banking accounts; goods and material values and other property elements which may be sold and included in sum for discharge of loan debt.

QUOTA 51481431971941 – Share of participation in mutual volume of production and sales of goods and services of each participant of monopoly association.

QUOTA OF CURRENT ASSETS 2185182194 - minimum amount of money necessary to the enterprise (firm) to meet general working capital requirements.

QUOTA OF CURRENT ASSETS AT INCOMPLETE PRODUCTION 56482131981 - cost of products which are at different stages of the production process, from the start of production to the finished product.

R

RATE 719 684219 817 - the established amount of payment for payment, rent of property, wages, insurance payment, etc.

RATE OF DEPOSIT 519312619712 – interest rate that is payable under a deposit by bank.

RATE OF DEPRECIATION 48971851947 – Percentage or fixed rate per cent of the book value of fixed assets per year.

RATE OF EXCHANGE 18942149718516 – quantity of monetary or currency units of one country needed for acquisition of monetary units of another country.

RATE OF PIECE CALCULATION TIME 519418313184 - standard of time required to manufacture a unit of output, and of set-up time.

RATE OF SURPLUS VALUE 1431651481 - the ratio of surplus value appropriated by producers (profit) to the cost of reproduction of the labor force (worker wage), or the ratio of surplus labor time, during which all add value to the time required, with which the labor force is reproduced itself, expressing as a percentage.

RATE OF TIME 61431281989 - The estimated rate of time (in hours or minutes) required to perform a specific job (operations) in the set of organizational and technical conditions of operating enterprises (firms).

RATIO 48951721981 - technical-economic indicator reflecting limit value of parameter, the level of resource usage.

RATIONAL EMPLOYMENT 5987248949 - quantitative and qualitative composition of the organization's personnel, ensuring the fullest use of labor resources.

RATIONING OF MATERIAL RESOURCES 21967149851 - establishment of the maximum permissible amount of raw materials and materials necessary for the production of products.

RATIONALIZATION OF PRODUCTION 54874219821 - a set of organizational and technical measures that provide an improvement in the performance of the enterprise, for example, an increase in profit and profitability, a decrease in labor intensity and current production costs, an increase in the volume of production and an increase in product quality, etc.

RAW MATERIALS 798548 498617 - is a cost article that reflects the cost of the main materials and materials that are an integral part of the product, as well as the cost of auxiliary materials used in the production process of the product.

REAL AMOUNT 69431751947 - buyer solvency adjusted in terms of inflation.

REAL ESTATE 564812319712 – land, buildings, structures and other capital construction objects built on them owned by the state, individuals or legal entities.

REAL INVESTMENTS 89851498647 - investment in the material production industry to increase fixed capital and increase production stocks.

REAL MONEY FLOW 619 71421841 - the difference between the inflow and outflow of funds from investment and operational activities in each period of capital investments.

REAL MONEY FLOW 619 71421841 - the difference between the inflow and outflow of funds from investment and operational activities in each period of capital investments.

RECEIPTS FROM SALES 614821319718 – monetary sum received on account of an enterprise for sales of products and rendering of services.

RECIPIENT 71971848947 - is a legal or physical person receiving payments, income; a recipient is also understood as a country attracting foreign investment.

RECONSTRUCTION OF THE ENTERPRISE 64851721981 - directing of capital construction, providing for the implementation of a complex of construction and installation measures for the radical restructuring of the enterprise on the basis of expanding and improving the layout of production areas and re-equipping them with new productive equipment and advanced technology.

RECORDS MANAGEMENT 516489498517 - operations related to the passage of business papers (documents) and carried out by the administrative and management apparatus of the enterprise.

REENGINEERING 49131856471 - activities for the improvement and restructuring of existing technical and technological solutions at production facilities.

REFACTION 57849831961 - reduction in the price of products sold as a result of non-compliance of their consumer properties with the requirements of the buyer; deviation from the technical conditions provided for in the contract.

REGIME (NOMINAL) TIME FUND 489514898617 - the operating time of a unit of equipment at its maximum use in the planning period, defined as the product of the number of working days in the planning period by the number of working shifts and the number of hours per shift.

REGIONAL MARKET 61871421847 - the market of a specific product (service) that is sold in a certain area (region).

REGRESSIVE TAXATION 69871231947 – Taxes, the rate of which falls while the total income rises.

REGULATION OF THE MARKET ECONOMY 549516938714 - measures of influence on the economy by state impact through tax policy, system of subsidies and benefits, changes in the interest rate for the loan, increase insecurity in state orders.

REGULATION OF THE MARKET ECONOMY 549516938714 - measures of influence on the economy by state impact through tax policy, system of subsidies and benefits, changes in the interest rate for the loan, increase insecurity in state orders.

REGULATORY DEVICES AND DEVICES 548697498 - are an integral part of the main production backgrounds.

REJECTION 618471318684 – Established by official commission of a fraction defective as a result of discovered deviations from approved standards or from technical specifications.

REINVESTMENTS 896514312817 - use of income from investment transactions to advance new investments.

RELATED PRODUCTS 51648931971 - are products directly related to the consumption of basic products and affecting demand.

RELACIÓN 48951721981 - técnico-económica indicador que refleja el valor límite del parámetro, el nivel de uso de recursos.

RELEASE OF WORKING CAPITAL 617514319421 – Result of rational use of working capital.

REMISSION 49131949871 - official permission to exempt from paying debt, tax or penalty (fine).

RENT 49718016541 - temporary transfer by the owner of the property (lessor) of the legal right to use land, buildings, structures, tools and other active elements of fixed assets to another person (tenant).

RENT 31848561 – Assignment for the temporary use of the property for a set fee.

RENT «by lessee» **71931851481** – Fee to be paid by lessee for right of property use taken under a lease.

RENT «income received» 54931481971 - income received by the owner from the use of capital without his participation in entrepreneurial activities, leased property, etc.

RENT FROM NATURAL RESOURCE POTENTIAL 428516317418 - is the most effective form of taxation.

RENTAL FEE 71931851481 - remuneration paid by the tenant for the right to use the leased property.

RENTING 498317818471 - short-term rental of machinery and equipment without the right of their subsequent purchase - rent.

RENOVATION 21947131967 - the procedure for replacing physically worn and obsolete equipment with similar or more advanced equipment.

RENTER 371491 – Hiring party which provides for a cash consideration the hiring property for temporary use by a hirer.

RENTIER 48131781984 - is an individual living on receiving interest on monetary capital loaned or on securities income.

REORGANIZATION 84951751849 - is a system of measures for restructuring, transformation of the enterprise, company.

REPAIR OF MAIN PRODUCTION FUNDS 61421721854 - organizational and technical measures to ensure the operability of equipment, machines by replacing or repairing failed parts and assemblies, as well as carrying out current and major repairs of buildings, structures, etc.

REPAYMENT FUND 319714219816 - is a fund created to repay monetary obligations, update major production funds, issue shares that are collateral upon receipt of a loan, etc.

REPORT 798 612319718 - is a document reflecting the result of the work done over a specified period of time.

REPRODUCTION 514128719 914 – is a continuous implementation of the process of production of material goods, which in terms of natural and material composition reflect the means of production and consumer goods produced during the year. There is a difference between simple and extended reproduction.

RESEARCH AND DEVELOPMENT (R&D) 69871481 - activities of research, development organizations and relevant divisions of the enterprise involved in theoretical, experimental, scientific research and development for the creation of new products and advanced technology, taking into account the use of the achievements of scientific and technological progress, improvement of the organization and management of production.

RESERVE EQUIPMENT 517218516214 - is part of the fleet of installed equipment under scheduled repair or reserve.

RESERVE FUND 519317419814 - is a fund that is created to repay current payments of an enterprise in the event that a number of profits does not provide full cash turnover with the expansion of fixed assets and an increase in working capital.

RESERVE STOCKS 564 712819 49 – reserves prepared for cases of inopportune coming of current supply for instance when interval between two deliveries is more than planned one.

RESOURCE SAVING 598148514217 48 - intensification of production through organizational and technical measures: introduction of achievements of scientific and technical progress, rational use of material and labor resources.

RESIDUAL VALUE 648514518711 - is a part of the value of fixed assets that is not transferred to finished products as a result of early termination of operation of these funds and their write-off from the balance sheet of the enterprise.

RETAIL 498712674918 - activities for the sale of goods and services in the domestic market to the population, i.e., to the end user for personal use.

RETURN ON CAPITAL INVESTMENTS 51849131948 - is the period during which advance capital investments are reimbursed by profit (increase in profits) received as a result of savings from capital investments.

RETURN ON CAPITAL INVESTMENTS WITH DISCOUNT VOLUME 519 617219 714 - the period during which advance capital investments pay off with the income received at the estimated discount rate.

RETIREMENT OF EQUIPMENT 691318714217 - Writing-off of physically worn out and obsolescent equipment from the enterprise balance.

RETROFIT INSTALLATION 548164918 - Improvement, upgrading of equipment, machines, processes, in order to increase productivity and to improve their economic performance.

REQUISITION 89451821964 - transfer or temporary seizure of property of an individual or legal entity by order of state bodies.

REVALUATION OF PROPERTY 219613819714 - a change in the book value of the property compared to its original value, for example, as a result of inflation.

REVERSE 47931851478 - property returned to the original owner.

RHYTHMICS OF PRODUCTION 61971231948 - uniform output at time intervals (hour, shift, day, decade, etc.) as a result of organizational work at the enterprise.

RISK 549121 498 - the probability of losses resulting from unforeseen adverse conditions.

RISK ANALYSIS 819498519614 - study of possible causes of material or financial losses as a consequence of an unforeseen change in the economic situation.

RISK AND UNCERTAINTY FACTORS 714 893219 618 - factors that are taken into account in the calculations of capital investment efficiency under various project implementation conditions. The following methods are used.

RISK CAPITAL 51481291948 - advance payment of tender funds to research and development, the impact of which can be problematic, i.e., it can't always bring enough time.

RISK INDICATOR 564841 - calculated value of estimated losses in the transition to the production of new commodities, attributed to the profit from their sales.

RISK FACTOR 564841 - is the estimated value of the expected losses during the transition to the production of new products, attributed to the profit from its sale.

RISK MANAGEMENT 719 649818 716 - a list of organizational and technical measures designed to reduce the risk of operations.

RISK MINIMIZATION 61421851961 - is a set of organizations, technical and economic and management measures aimed at reducing risk in the process of financial, economic and production activities.

RISK PERCENTAGE 81971854961 - the possibility of the investor's failure due to a change in the interest rate in the market.

ROYALTY 514891619714 - periodic payment to the licensor for the right to use inventions, patents, know-how, etc. established in the license agreement.

S

SALARY 914 489198 71 - is a value category that characterizes the transformed form of value and the price of labor; the form of distribution of part of the value between workers in accordance with their share of participation in total social work.

SALARY SAVINGS 561498519712 - is an economy achieved as a result of reduced labor intensity, i.e., time per unit production.

SALES 718 648519 71 - a set of measures to ensure the sale of finished products.

SALES CHANNEL 318481499417 - methods of delivery of goods on time from the producer to the consumer.

SALES LOGISTICS 619 217218 47 - is an integral part of the general logistics system, which performs market research functions (marketing), which are carried out by legal entities and individuals and ensure the promotion of goods from the manufacturer to the buyer with the transfer of legal ownership of the purchased goods.

SALES INCENTIVE 54831721947 - a set of organizational measures that stimulate the growth of demand in the sale of goods (services).

SALES VOLUME 497 814 - the number of sales.

SANCTIONS 514319 618 - economic measures providing for moral or material punishment of physical and legal entities for violation of the terms of the contract, agreement.

SANITATION 648 894988 71 - a system of state and banking measures to prevent bankruptcy of large industrial enterprises or improve their financial situation in the context of economic crisis (revaluation of property, loans, subsidies, etc.).

SANITIZATION 498 69419871 - prevention of debt insolvency (bankruptcy) through the issuance of securities.

SAVINGS 59421849871 - is a system of organizational and technical measures aimed at the rational use of material, labor and monetary resources in the process of production of inventory.

SAVINGS GROWTH RATE 514 916317 819 - the value of the decrease in the increase in costs attributed to the cost of growth in the exchange of production.

SAVINGS OF MATERIAL AND ENERGY RESOURCES 564189498712 - savings achieved as a result of measures to improve the use of material and energy resources.

SAVINGS ON CONDITIONAL COSTS 498716219714 - savings achieved by increasing production volume.

SAVINGS ON DEPRECIATION 219314218711 - savings that are achieved in the result of improving the use of an effective time fund for the development of equipment.

SAY'S LAW 48148131947 – the law states that introduction of new goods in the market creates demand for the goods; the same also applies to the rendering of new services. Supply and demand are in balance constantly.

SECURITIES 317518319417 - documentary evidence giving property rights and the right to receive Income to their owner. Securities include shares, bonds of companies and enterprises, as well as bonds of state loans; promissory notes, etc.

SECONDARY DEMAND 317 694 318 817 - demand for goods that depends directly on the demand for another product.

SELF-FINANCING 619 818319 71 - is a financial and economic activity in which all current expenses for simple and expanded reproduction are reimbursed from their own sources.

SELF-SUFFICIENCY 498 712819 49 - the principle of effective operation of the enterprise, firm, according to which all the costs incurred for simple reproduction should be covered by income (revenue) from the sale of manufactured products.

SELLER'S MARKET 71948951964 - is an economic situation in the market in which prices rise as a result of a shortage of goods, i.e., the value of demand at current prices exceeds the value of supply.

SELLER PRICE 319 684219 81 - price limit below which the manufacturer will not be able to get a minimum profit.

SEMI-FINISHED PRODUCTS 614 712514 51 - is a product of labor that has not passed all technological stages (operations) to turn it into final products.

SEPARATISM 941 319841 21 - is a regional economic policy that provides for the creation of a market independent of the center.

SEQUESTER 319842 197 - state restriction or restriction on the use of property.

SERIAL PRODUCTION 649 124 489 71 - production of a certain nomenclature of structurally similar products in small batches (series) and with the established frequency of their re-release.

SERVICES 4931518641491 - types of work as a result of labor non-production activities of an individual or legal entity in order to meet certain needs of bathers (customers).

SERVICE LIFE OF EQUIPMENT 574 481319 614 - period from the beginning of operation of the equipment (beginning of the depreciation period) to its complete physical wear and tear (completion of the amortization period).

SERVICE SPHERE 648314219715 - provision of material and non-material services by various sectors of the national economy.

SCIENTIFIC AND TECHNICAL ACTIVITY OF THE ENTERPRISE 618317519714 - is an activity that is mainly reduced to applied research and is the stage in the life cycle of a product or technological process when, based on the results of fundamental or own research, the idea of a new product or technological process is developed and prepared for the implementation.

SCIENTIFIC AND TECHNICAL POTENTIAL 56131957841 - is the result of the implementation of scientific and technical achievements in the field of industrial production and scientific and technical organizations.

SCIENTIFIC AND TECHNICAL PROGRESS 564817319418 - is the purposeful use of advanced achievements of science and technology in production in order to improve the efficiency and quality of production processes, better meet the needs of society.

SCIENTIFIC AND TECHNICAL PRODUCTS 69831971871 - are the results of intellectual work aimed at improving production efficiency.

SHADOW INCOME 314819319618 - income of a legal entity or individual from participation in a shadow economic activity.

SHARE 617319819491 - is a security certifying the right to receive part of the profit in the form of dividends.

SHARE CAPITAL 694182548471 - is capital, the source of which is the unification of individual capital through the issuance and sale of securities. The growth of equity capital is achieved as a result of the use of part of the profit and issue of shares and bonds.

SHORT-TERM CREDIT 564 718914 818 - Credit assignable for provision of excessive raw material and material stock, of timely paid salary, of temporary replenishment of own circulation assets shortage and also of implementation of new equipment and new technology under condition of their paying-off in one year.

SHORT-TERM LOAN 564 718914 818 - is a loan provided to provide excess stocks of raw materials and materials, for timely payment of wages and temporary replenishment of the lack of own working capital, as well as for the introduction of new equipment, technology, provided that it is repaid within one year.

SHIFT FACTOR 589 842819 64 - is an indicator of the assessment of the intended use of equipment operating time, which is calculated as the ratio of the number of machine tools worked during the day to the total number of installed equipment.

SCHEDULING 318614 718512 - Coordination of established included all fulfilled operations consequence of operative control process of industrial enterprise production activity.

SCIENTIFIC AND TECHNICAL ACTIVITY OF ENTERPRISE 618317519714 - Activity, which is largely confined to applied research and is the stage in the life cycle of a product or process, when the results of fundamental or on-site research designed and prepared to introduce the idea of a new product or process.

SCIENTIFIC AND TECHNICAL POTENTIAL 56131957841 - The result of the implementation of scientific and technological achievements in the sphere of material production and scientific and technical organizations.

SCIENTIFIC AND TECHNICAL PRODUCT 69831971871 - Results of intellectual work aimed at improving the efficiency of production.

SHADOW ECONOMY 51621831949 - is a part of the country's economy in which there is no public control over the production, distribution, exchange and consumption of material goods.

SMALL ENTERPRISE 718421894851 - is a small enterprise of any form of ownership, characterized primarily by a limited number of employees; the most effective form of small business organization in market conditions.

SIMULTANEOUS OPERATION OF SEVERAL MACHINES 5485491941 – The work of one worker, machine operator on two or more machines. It helps to reduce downtime of full shifts, to increase productivity.

SINECURE 316 284919 61 - figuratively a well-paid position with minimal labor costs.

SINGLE (INDIVIDUAL) PRODUCTION 519612719491 - type of organization of production for the manufacture of products of limited consumption (piece products).

SINGLE ELASTICITY 316548919217 – condition under which sales revenue for certain goods stays invariable that is rate of sales volumes' growth (decrease) equals rate of decrease (growth) of price.

SMALL ENTERPRISE 718421894851 – Any small business ownership, characterized primarily by a limited number of employees, the most effective form of small business in a market economy.

SOCIEDAD ANÓNIMA (JOINT-STOCK COMPANY (JSC)) 5163184101482 – Negocio cuyos propietarios son un grupo de personas que tienen acciones en una empresa u organización. Empresa compuesta por personas físicas, jurídicas o capitales individuales que son la base para la creación de fondos autorizados, mediante la emisión de acciones, bonos, etc. con el propósito de tener activos productivos (capital) y capital de trabajo (capital flotante).

SOCIAL PARTNERSHIP 518 649319 712 - protection of institutions in social and labor relations.

SOCIAL SPHERE 498 479 819 617 - sectors of the national economy that do not participate in material production, but ensure the organization of service, exchange, distribution and consumption of goods, as well as the formation of the standard of living of the population, its well-being.

SOFT CREDIT 618 471219 714 – Credit given on a preferable basis i.e., with lesser interest rate and with more continuous term of the taken sum acquittal.

SOLD PRODUCTS 54121381948 - the volume of finished products sold on the side and paid for by the buyer.

SOLID PRICE 574 617217 914 - price permanently valid throughout the term of the agreement, for example, the price of the delivered goods.

SOLIDARITY 49851749854 - personal responsibility for the implementation of tasks in solving social and labor problems.

SOLVENCY 574 7814981 48 - the ability of physical or legal entities to fully fulfill their payment obligations within the established period.

SOLVENT DEMAND 819 71249141 - funds of buyers (consumers) that ensure the ability to pay for their needs for material goods and services.

SOLVENCY THEORY 619 71481851 - is a taxation theory that provides for an increase in the tax rate as the taxpayer's income grows.

SPECIFIC CAPITAL INVESTMENTS 491 711498481 - the value of one-time costs per unit of annual increase in production volume or per unit of growth of fixed assets.

SPECIFIC CURRENT COSTS 698491317 485 - current production costs per unit of production.

SPECIFIC FUND CAPACITY OF A UNIT OF PRODUCT OR SERVICE 514 718517 485 - is an indicator reflecting the cost of fixed assets per unit of product or service.

SPECIFIC FUND CAPACITY OF EQUIPMENT 471 318318471 498 - is an indicator reflecting the cost of fixed assets, which falls on 1 hour of the main operation of the equipment.

SPECIFIC FUND CAPACITY OF THE UNIT OF PRODUCT NORMATIVE 548 671319 781 - is an indicator that is developed on the basis of economic and mathematical modeling, which allows to assess the impact of production facts-arguments on its value in separate intervals of the prospective period.

SPECIFIC WEIGHT OF THE ACTIVE PART OF THE MAIN PRODUCTION FUNDS 549 647498 61 - is the share of the value of fixed assets attributable to the active part, which is the leading part and serves as the basis for assessing the technical level and production capacity.

SPECIFICATION 317 498479 641 - is a document that reflects a list of parts and assemblies of the manufactured product, indicating its weight, material used, quantity per unit of finished product.

SPECIALIZATION SUBTAL 698 714 218 718 - independent production of parts, assemblies that are used in the far range to complete finished products. For example, the bearing industry.

SPECIALIZATION SUBJECT 698 749219 814 - additional production of a certain nomenclature of products intended for various sectors of the national economy.

SPECIALIZATION OF PRODUCTION 614 712819 716 - is a form of organization of production based on the division of works.

SPECIALIZATION TECHNOLOGICAL 319 684218 712 - creation of separate independent enterprises to perform individual stages or operations of the technological process of production.

SPECIALTY 498 682319 497 - specialization of labor activity within a particular profession, providing for the availability of special knowledge, education, experience.

STABILIZATION OF THE ECONOMY 318 648219 671 - restoration of the country's economy (economy) after the crisis; a state that meets the interests of all segments of society

STAFF FLOW 519 614 - reduction in the number of employees of the enterprise (institution) as a result of their dismissal for one reason or another. The turnover rate of workers is defined as the ratio of the number of dismissed to the average number of employees.

STAFF FLOW RATE 49849148 - the number of dismissed during the year, classified as the average number of employees.

STAGFLATION 497 248598 641 - the state of the economy, including stagnation and increasing inflationary process.

STAGNATION 498 648319 217 - economic situation in the country, reflecting the suspension of growth or fall in production with a decrease in the number of employees (increase in unemployment).

STANDARD 5713196194 – Sample, measure, the maximum rate or amount set by the measure.

STANDARD «norms and requirements» 749 319498 218 - is a regulatory and technical document that establishes norms and requirements for quality and measurement parameters of labor items and products. Used as a reference for mapping.

STANDARD OF FINISHED PRODUCTS 39861429871 - time for selection, packaging, accumulation of products to transit norms, delivery, etc.; in value terms - the need for working capital for storing stocks of finished products.

STANDARDIZATION 648 217319 641 - introduction of unified state norms and requirements, which are a prerequisite for producers and allow to reduce the range of products produced in the direction of further specialization of production.

STANDARD OF BEHAVIOR ON MARKET 69831729851 - absence of coercive methods of competition and of collusions among manufacturers presented on the market. It is distinguished by growing demand for a wide range of products.

STATE BUDGET 598618517544 - is a balanced list of income and expenses developed, approved and regulated by legislative and executive authorities.

STATE ANTIMONOPOLY POLICY 59831849714 - is a government policy aimed at developing competition and creating restrictions on the monopoly activities of participants working in market relations.

STATE LOAN 564812318497 - is a type of credit and financial operations aimed at temporarily replenishing the state budget at the expense of a loan.

STATE REGULATION OF PRICES 51851491812 - Direct state participation in retail prices fixing.

STATE RESEARCH AND TECHNOLOGY POLICY 318516319712 - constituent of social and economical policy which expresses governmental interest toward scientific and technological activity.

STATE RETAIL PRICE 584 698319 81 - is the final price at which consumer goods and non-which tools and labor items are sold through the trading network.

STATE PRICE 519498 714 - price set by state bodies.

STATE SECTOR 589712694318 – constituent of national economy denoted the state deals which provide state with profit according to current taxation legislation.

STATUTE 498318485481 - charter, regulations on the rights and obligations of an individual or legal entity.

STATUTORY FUND OF THE ENTERPRISE 649 748219 817 - the basis for the formation of fixed assets and working capital of the enterprise at the expense of budget allocations, funds of founders and participants, mutual funds.

STIMULATING MARKETING 498614219517 - market conditions when there is no demand for certain goods and services, i.e., supply is not realized.

STOCK 317518319417 – Documentary proof giving a property right for acquisition of income to its holder. Bonds and shares of companies and enterprises as also public bonds; promissory notes and so on.

STOCK EXCHANGE 49831721947 - is a constantly functioning market where shares, bonds and other securities are bought and sold.

STOCK CAPITAL 694182548471 – Capital the formation source of which is to be individual capitals' unification by means of issuing and sales of securities. Growth of joint stock is achieved through use of profit part of stock and shares emission.

STOCKS CURRENT 671 814218 17 - is the main type of normalized reserves, which are defined as the product of the average accurate consumption of labor items for the interval between two rates.

STOCKS OF GOODS 514812319481 - intended for sale finished products and other material values located in the warehouse of the enterprise, in sales and trade organizations.

SPHERE OF MATERIAL PRODUCTION 497 148219 6143172194 - a complex of branches of the national economy that produce and sell material production products (industrial products, agriculture, etc.), including the provision of material services for supply, purchase and sale, etc.

STRATEGIC LEVEL OF BRAND MANAGEMENT 694 217319 848 - quantitative assessment of potential buyers, with the help of which the goals and objectives of the enterprise are formed to meet the needs of potential buyers, the need for material and technical resources for the implementation of planned activities is ensured, strategy recommendations aimed at ensuring the most favorable commercial activities are developed.

STRATEGIC MARKETING 498 671481 216 - is a condition for the timely provision of the relevant market with certain goods with a specified volume of supplies.

STRATEGIC MANAGEMENT 519 642719 518 - is the process of developing long-term goals and objectives related to the formation of a promising production program (order portfolios, provision of financial, material, labor resources), establishment and maintenance of relationships with suppliers of material resources and consumers of manufactured products (services), commodity markets and labor exchanges, etc.

STRATEGIC PLANNING 318 614514 41 - direction of planning the economic activities of the enterprise, taking into account changes in the external and internal environment, real assessment of opportunities to take its place in the relevant markets, ensuring the planned level of production efficiency.

STRATEGIC PERSONNEL MANAGEMENT 719 642519 684 - management of the formation of a labor potential of an organization that meets the requirements of a market economy and provides an appropriate level of competitiveness of employees of the enterprise and the production process (Equipment of human resources of appropriate qualification), taking into account constant changes in the economy and legal regulation, establishment of relations and interaction with organizations that supply material resources and contribute to the sale of finished products and services, as well as changes in the external environment.

STORAGE OF MATERIALS 497518219681 - is a complex of organizational and technical measures to prevent the loss of qualitative and quantitative characteristics of materials in warehouses.

STRUCTURAL SHIFTS 64851331849 - a change in the share of a particular nomenclature position of products as a result of increasing the volume of highly profitable products, removing from production or reducing the volume of production of outdated and uncompetitive products.

STRUCTURES 598748319 71 - is an integral passive part of the main production assets, including engineering and construction facilities necessary for the production process and not related to the change of labor objects (pumping stations, tunnels, bridges, etc.).

STRUCTURE OF CURRENT COSTS BY TYPE OF COST
 498 317316 21 - the share of costs that vary depending on the volume of production (variable costs), i.e., the share of raw materials, basic materials (including components), energy for technological purposes, wages of the main production workers.

STRUCTURE OF MAIN PRODUCTION BACKGROUNDS
814 641319 71 - share of the cost of each classification group in their total value.

SUBRENAL 194 471 - transfer by the tenant of part of the leased property to a third party. The right to sublease is provided for in the lease agreement.

SUBSIDIARY 548168498184 - is a legally independent joint-stock company whose controlling stake belongs to another joint-stock company.

SUBSIDY 319418719491 – irrevocable budget subsidy (help) giving out to enterprises, institutions, enterprises for reimbursement of losses from production and sales of product as well for support of relatively low retail prices for separate consumer goods.

SUBSTITUE GOODS 214817218516 – Goods that can be used to satisfy partly or fully the same needs of buyers in comparison with basic product.

SUPER-LONG PERIOD 619 543819 71 - is a hypothetical period of time in supply theory, which involves the possibility of changing (improving) existing technological processes of production based on the introduction of achievements of scientific and technological progress.

SUPER PROFIT 497 81681947 - excess of actual profit over planned or average value.

SUPPLEMENTARY REMUNERATION 689 718514371 – pay-offs provided by legislation and labor contract for instance payment for regular and additional vacations.

SUPPLIER 4981751 - is an individual or legal entity that ensures the supply of inventory for the production of goods (services).

SUPPLY AND DEMAND 47961251948 - are two main and opposite characteristics of the (commodity) market economy.

SUPPLY AND DEMAND BALANCE 471819514317 - is one of the conditions for regulating a market economy, which reflects the compliance of the volume of production with the structure of demand.

SUPPLY CURVE 489 471819 498 – Curve graphically describing supply law according to which along with an increase of a price a supply rises.

SUPPLY FACTORS 491 617318 78 - factors affecting the cost of goods presented on the market, i.e., the cost of resources, efficiency of technological processes, taxes and benefits, competitiveness and prices for similar goods.

SUPPLY THEORY 485 648498 71 - is an integral part of the economic theory of the market; explores the causes and conditions affecting the formation of supply in the market of goods and services.

SURCHARGE RATE 71431651481 - the ratio of the surplus value assigned by the producer (profit) to the cost of labor reproduction (worker's wages) or the ratio of surplus labor during which surplus value is created to the required time by which the labor force itself is reproduced; expressed as a percentage.

SURPLUS FOR BUYER 498514598317 – Difference between actual payment for goods and estimated one.

SURPLUS FOR MANUFACTURER 56849131891 - Additional benefit gained as a result of cost rise.

SUSTAINABLE PASSIVES 497 618319 737 - are part of the working capital not owned by the enterprise, but at its disposal.

SYNDICATE 319 894218 71 - is an association of enterprises that produce homogeneous products, created for joint commercial activities in order to reduce tensions in competition and generate higher income (were) while maintaining full independence.

T

TABLE ACCOUNTING 548 617219 617 - daily accounting of time of the work of each employee of the enterprise.

TACTICAL PLANNING 497 674898 491 - development of plans for the distribution of resources of the enterprise in the process of implementing strategic goals.

TARIFFS 549718 649 714 - is a system of officially established rates at which enterprises pay for various production and consumer services, such as wage rates, transport tariffs.

TARIFF GRID 497 678498 741 - list of rates for wages.

TARIFFICATION OF WORKS 748 671219 817 - establishment of tariffs for services and wage rates.

TARGET MARKETING 51631421949 - economically justified selection of segments with a list of products for each segment.

TAX

TAX BASE 718481061498 - a set of income of individuals or legal entities subject to taxation.

TAX BENEFIT 64851731941 - full or partial tax exemption of individuals or legal entities.

TAX CONCESSIONS 64851731941 - Full or partial exemption from taxation of individuals or legal entities.

TAX DECLARATION 689317519481 - is an official documentary statement of the taxpayer (individual or legal entity) on the total income received during the determined period (year) and on tax rebates and benefits established by law.

TAX - DIRECT TAX 4864728941 - mandatory payments to the budget established by the legislation, which are levied on the proceeds or property of legal entities and individuals.

INDIRECT TAX 42131931781 - tax on goods and services, which is established in the form of allowances to the prices of goods or tariffs for services.

TAX REGULATION 58971231947 - measures of the state's environmental impact on the economy, economic and social processes by changing tax policy (tightening of tax rates, introduction of additional benefits) to stimulate production efficiency.

TAX SANCTIONS 514217 - a set of methods and means of influencing individuals and legal entities that have violated the current legislation on taxation.

TAXATION 31971851641 - is the process of establishing and collecting taxes paid to the budget by individuals and legal entities on the basis of the current system of taxes and tax rates established by law.

TAXATION REGRESSIVE «decreases» 69871231947 - taxes, the rate of which decreases as total income grows.

TAXATION PROPORTIONAL 61931851971 - taxation providing for a single tax rate regardless of the total income of an individual or legal entity.

TAXES 271318371478 - mandatory payments collected by central and local public authorities from individuals and legal entities received by the state and local budgets.

TAXABLE INCOME 319618318417 - gross income of an entity, firm, institution and other taxpayers, reduced by the amount of gross tax-exempt income in accordance with the current law on benefits and discounts.

TAX ON THE PROPERTY OF ENTERPRISES 49871271941 – fixed

TAXATION PROGRESSIVE 59864131971 - taxation, which provides for an increase in tax rates as the total income of the payer grows.

TAX REGULATIONS 58971231947 – Measure of indirect effects of the state on the economy, economic and social processes through changes in tax policy (tightening of tax rates, the introduction of additional benefits) to encourage production efficiency.

TAX SACTION 514217 – Combination of methods and means of influence on individuals and entities which violate the legislation on taxation.

TAX STATEMENT 689317519481 – official taxpayer (corporate body or individual) documentary tax statement on integral income received over a certain period (year) and established by current legislation tax abatements and exemptions covering it.

TAXABLE INCOME «to current legislation» 319618318417 – Gross income of enterprise, firm, institution and other taxpayers, decreased by sum of gross income which is released from taxes according to current legislation on allowances and discounts.

TAXABLE INCOME 571498 497 - is a part of the gross income of individuals or legal entities, which serves as the basis for calculating mandatory payments to the budget.

TAXATION 31971851641 – Process of establishing and collecting taxes to be made in the budget by individuals and entities on the basis of the current system of taxes and tax rates set by the legislation.

TAXES 271318371478 – Mandatory payments levied by central and local governments on individuals and businesses; coming to the state and local budgets.

ENTERPRISE PROPERTY TAX 49871271941 - fixed assets, intangible assets, stocks and expenses on the payer's balance sheet are taxed.

INCOME TAX 491819317481 - is a component of the balance sheet profit, which serves as a source of redistribution of national income.

INCOME TAX « main type of direct ta» 42851748948 - is the main type of direct tax, which is levied on the income or profit of the enterprise and goes to the revenue part of the budget.

PROGRESSIVE TAXATION 59864131971 – Taxation, providing higher tax rates to the extent of the growth of the total income of the payer.

PROFIT TAX 491819317481 – Is an integral part of retained earnings, which is the source of the redistribution of national income.

PROFIT TAXABLE 31851431961 - gross or balance profit reduced by the amount of preferential profit.

PROPORTIONAL TAXATION 61931851971 – Taxation, providing a unified tax rate regardless of the total income of the physical or legal person.

REGRESSIVE TAXATION 69871231947 - Taxes, the rate of which falls while the total income rises.

VALUE ADDED TAX (VAT) 491316318914 - tax is the rate of withdrawal to the bill of part of value added created at all stages of production of goods, performance of work or provision of services.

TECHNICAL AND ECONOMIC INDICATORS 519 617218 419 - a system of planned or accounting indicators reflecting production volumes in physical and value terms, use of material and labor resources, means of production, such as the cost of gross or commercial products, fund return, production, duration of turnover.

TECHNICAL RE-ARMAMENT 518 617219 718 - is a system of organizational and technical measures, providing for the introduction of achievements of scientific and technological progress aimed at improving the fleet of basic technological equipment, existing technology, replacing physically worn-out and obsolete equipment, eliminating bottlenecks in the production process.

TECHNOLOGICAL EQUIPMENT 514 812498 714 - various groups of devices characterized by dozens of items, i.e., devices designed to establish and fix workpieces in the required position regarding the working bodies of the machine and cutting tools.

TECHNOLOGICAL STOCKS (PREPARATORY) 564 947948 41 - stocks that are created in cases where the incoming material values do not meet the requirements of the technological process and are treated accordingly before being put into production (drying, corrosion removal, etc.).

TECHNOLOGICAL PREPARATION OF PRODUCTION 518 617219 498 - organizational principle of distribution of assignments (works) for the preliminary development of standard and promising technological processes that reflect the consistent the complexity of technological operations for the manufacture of planned products.

TECHNOLOGICAL WASTE 549 617219 814 - import-free inevitable waste. At the stage of technological preparation of production, this waste is minimized as a result of technical preparation of the material for production consumption.

TECHNOLOGY 614 812498 798 - a set of consistent operations performed in the process of manufacturing goods (delivery of service).

TENDER 189 417218 489 - a competitive form of placing applications for the supply of inventory and performance of contract works in order to ensure cost-effective conditions for their implementation.

TERM OF FULL REPAYMENT OF DEBT 498 217317 49 - is an additional indicator of the effectiveness of the investment project.

TESTING OF QUALITY 598 712894 716 – Evaluation of compliance of actual performance figures of goods defined their suitability for consumption, characteristics, approved specifications, standards or customer requirements.

THE COEFFICIENT OF ELASTICY 518 619419 714 – percentage change in the quantity of goods sold per one percent change in the price of goods (products).

THE REAL SECTOR OF THE ECONOMY 51731964851 - is the production of competitive and high-tech products that allow to satisfy the interests of consumers in the domestic and foreign markets.

THE RATIO OF THE TOTAL COST OF SALES AND BATHROOM PRODUCTS TO REVENUE 514 712618518 - is still a thing reflecting the change in the profitability of the enterprise.

THE CRITERION OF ACCEPTANCE OF INVESTMENT PROJECT 548712317491 - is the surplus of accumulated real money in any time interval in which this participant carries out costs or receives income.

THE RIGHT OF OPERATIONAL MANAGEMENT 5714988 - is the right to own, use and dispose of property granted to a state enterprise and organizations in accordance with the current legislation of the Russian Federation.

THE PRICE OF NEW PRODUCTS 219 684 888 717 - is the upper limit of the price of a new product or the conditionally maximum price of a new product, at which production and consumption are of the same benefit to both the manufacturer and the consumer.

THE PRODUCT DEVELOPMENT AND IMPROVEMENT FUND 648317219498 - is a fund designed to finance the implementation of scientific and technical progress, update fixed assets, improve the organization of production, conduct research and development work, and carry out other organizational and technical activities.

THE PRODUCT MANAGER 619712894317 - is a natural or legal person who has the right to manage the movement of goods at its own discretion or with the permission of the commissioner.

TIME FACTOR 128491 649718 - is a factor that provides when calculating the efficiency of capital investments, the difference in the implementation of capital investments by one point in time.

TIME STANDARD 61431281989 - is the estimated norm of time (in hours or minutes) necessary to perform certain work (operation) in the specified organizational and technical conditions of the existing enterprise (firm).

TIMING 598498319718 - measurement of the employee's working time spent on the implementation of specified technological operations in order to establish the labor intensity of these operations.

TIPO DE IMPUESTOS INDIRECTOS (EXCISE) 518716319419819 – Tipo de impuestos indirectos – impuestos de consumo que son parte integral de la liberación de precios y que serán cargados al presupuesto completamente. Es para ser aplicado en bienes de consumo generalmente.

TOOLS 516 714 - are the main part of the means of production, i.e. machines, equipment that are directly involved in the production process.

TRADE REVENUE 614 318519 718 - proceeds from the sale of goods.

TRADING FIRM 648 317499 148 - is an organization that ensures the sale and delivery of tangible assets on the basis of a legally formalized agreement indicating commercial liability for deviation in delivery time and quantity of order units.

TRANSFER DEVICES 891491 - are elements of the main production assets, with the help of which energy of various types is transferred, as well as liquid and gaseous substances (oil pipelines, gas pipelines, etc.).

TRANSNATIONAL MONOPOLY 819 712498 714 - are the largest industrial and financial organizations with a high concentration of production and capital both inside and outside the country.

TRANSPORT FORWARDER 648 751319 48 - is a legal entity that transports tangible assets by its own transport, taking into account the interests of the customer, on the basis of current tariffs, ensuring the reliability of delivery of the package-order, timeliness of delivery, etc.

TRANSPORT LOGISTICS 648 712895 718 - is one of the functions of logistics, which is entrusted with the delivery of material values to the consumer.

TRANSPORTATION INVENTORY 56471981961 – (Tp3) are to be calculated similarly to reserve stocks.

TRANSPORT STOCKS 56471981961 - are calculated in the same way as insurance stocks.

TRIAL MARKETING 59871431841 - justification of the economic feasibility of winning a new market segment based on an average estimate of revenue from short-term sales of the implemented goods.

TRUST 949 612518 489 - is an association of several similar enterprises, in which its participants completely lose their commercial, production and legal independence.

TURNOVER 481 614217 498 - movement of goods in the field of circulation; valuation of sold and purchased goods for a certain period.

TURNOVER COEFFICIENTS 619 718419 71 - coefficients used to diagnose the financial position of the recipient enterprise.

TURNOVER OF THE COMPANY 498 617498714 - includes three stages: at the first stage, working capital from monetary form is transferred to commodity (production stocks, labor force is acquired), to the second - production stocks with the participation of tools and workers Forces turn into finished products; on the third - finished products are sold, funds are exempt from commodity form and again accept money.

TURNOVER RATE 619 718419 71 – coefficients used in the diagnosis of the financial condition of the recipient company.

TURNOVER RATE OF PERSONNEL 49849148 – Number of retired during the year divided by the average payroll number of employees.

TURNOVER OF WORKING CAPITAL 548 819319 617 - indicator of working capital use, reflecting the time of one turnover in days.

TYPES OF MARKETING RESEARCH 317589619714 – Research set for types of marketing activity: advertisement, analysis of market demand, supply, price formation, payment capacity and etc.

U

UNIT FUND CAPACITY 619314219498 - is an economic indicator used to determine the additional need for fixed assets.

UNDER-LOADING OF PRODUCTION CAPACITIES 48971231649 - target and intra-shift loss of operating time of the main technological equipment (accounted for production capacity), exceeding the planned value.

UNDERUTILIZATION OF PRODUCTIVE CAPACITY 48971231649 – loss of the whole shift time or part time of a shift of main equipment work (admitted in the calculation of production capacity), exceeding the planned value.

UNDIFFERETIAL MARKETING 48951631841 - simplified diagram of the sales of goods, when manufacturers supply the market with their product range and try to expand the circle of buyers through the use of the marketing service, while not reacting on the consumer interests.

UNEMPLOYMENT 318514517618 - is a socio-economic phenomenon caused by a decrease in the level of use of able-bodied population wishing to participate in social production.

UNDIFFERENTIATED MARKETING 48951631841 - a simplified scheme for the sale of goods, when the producer supplies its product range to the market, with the power of the marketing service tries to expand the range of buyers without responding to the interests of the consumer.

UNFINISHED PRODUCTION 594817319714 - partially finished products that have not completely passed all the technological operations provided for in the technical specifications for the creation of finished products.

UNIFICATION 518 316497 48 - organizational and technical measures to reduce the unreasonably large diversity of products and means of production, including reducing the number of their sizes and modifications by bringing them to uniformity in shape, size, structure.

UNIT ELASTICITY 316548919217 - is a condition under which the revenue from the sale of a certain product remains unchanged, i.e., the rate of growth (reduction) of sales is identical to the rate of decline (growth) of the price.

UNIT OF CAPITALIZATION 648518798417 - cost of basic production assets element (machines, equipment, premises, buildings and so on) put to account of investment expenditures.

UNIT OF POWER MEASURE 319617319489 - Statistical unit of measure for estimation of number of machines, equipment, devices, power of engines installed in machines and equipment for setting them in motion, performance (laboriousness, machining content and output).

UNITARY ENTERPRISE 649 317318 64 - is a state-owned commercial organization without ownership of property.

UNIVERSAL PREFERENCE SYSTEM 491719 819481 - customs benefits that are provided to underdeveloped and developing countries.

UTILIZATION RATE OF DIMENSIONAL PARAMETERS 514 617518 719 - is an indicator of the intensity of use of equipment, defined as the ratio in which in the numerator each term is the product of the dimensional input of the part on the load factor of the machine by parts of this interval, and in the denominator - the product of one of the dimensional parameters of the machine by its load factor.

USEFULNESS 648 712319 614 - the ability of goods or services to meet the needs of individuals or legal entities.

VACATION PRICE 894 317 218 491 - a type of wholesale price; the price at which the company releases, gives its goods to consumers; the price of products sold by procurement organizations.

VALUATION OF FIXED ASSETS 548317314811 - determination of the value of fixed assets. There are several types of valuation.

VALUE ADDED TAX (VAT) 491316318914 - tax is the rate of withdrawal to the bill of part of value added created at all stages of production of goods, performance of work or provision of services.

VALUATION OF PROPERTY 619317219498 - total costs for the formation of the entire set of basic production assets and working capital, as well as expenses on maintaining fixed assets in working condition.

VALUE AS NEW 49861271941 – This kind of value is made up of two parts. First -the cost of reproduction of the labor force, reflecting the socially necessary labor time, that is, the worker's part-time, which is spent on the reproduction of the equivalent labor costs and estimated by wage of the worker. Another large part, that is surplus time, is a source of creation of surplus value, which is entirely given to commodity producer.

VENTURE ETERPRISES 318514218617 – are small enterprises of knowledge-intensive industries specializing in the production of intellectual labor products, i.e., in the development and implementation of innovations.

VENTURE OPERATIONS 31861728971 – financial transactions carried out with a certain degree of risk.

W

WAGE OF PRODUCTION AND RELATED WORKERS 314516 719481 – salary which is to be paid for accomplishment of technology operations for product manufacturing.

WAREHOUSE 397 214218 64 - is a production facility in which inventory (raw materials, material, finished products, etc.) is stored and prepared for the technological process and sale is carried out.

WARRANT 318421398728 - is a document confirming the fact of acceptance of the goods for storage.

WASTE OF COMPETITION 519 612719 811 – Additional expenses not included in plan and intended to advertise consumer properties of goods for demand rise.

WHOLESALE 319 818719 6 - sale of large batches of goods to intermediaries for further resale.

WHOLESALE BATCH 319 628498 71 - is a batch of manufactured products, which is used in market relations to assess the speed of sale of goods on the market and establish a deviation between supply and demand.

WHOLESALE BUYER 719 748 - is an intermediary presenter who, on behalf of retailers, buys goods.

WHOLESALE INDUSTRY PRICE 491 318219 714 - the price of goods set in addition to the wholesale price of the enterprise.

WHOLESALE PRICE OF ENTERPRISE 894 671918 491 - the price of a service at which costs are reimbursed and provided.

WORKPLACE 519641918517 - is the primary link of the enterprise, organization or part of the area adapted for the employee to perform the planned task.

WORK SEASONAL 98948121971 - periodically performed work predetermined by natural and climatic conditions.

WORKING CAPITAL 371 821498317 - a set of material and cash necessary for the normal functioning of the production process and the sale of products.

WORKING CAPITAL «cycle and the cost» 698 714319 671 - is a part of working capital that is fully consumed in each production cycle and the cost of which is transferred to newly created products.

WORKING CAPITAL STANDARD 2185182194 - is the minimum amount of money needed by the enterprise (firm) to meet the total need for a working capital.

WORKING FORCE 619318519471 - physical and intellectual capabilities of the able-bodied population, which are used in the production of material goods and in the social sphere.

WORKING TIME 61931781949 - the duration of work established by the legislation.

WORKING SHIFT 58972489 48 - working hours, legalized by a legislative decree.

WORKING MACHINERY AND EQUIPMENT 598314219714 - is the main group of fixed assets related to active.

METHODS OF BUSINESS ADMINISTRATION

In the eternal technologies' development, we often have to act and work in the areas unknown earlier. Therefore, for the eternal development of technologies, small business is one of means to achieve the aim which includes coming to the transition level and then to a large business:
419 819 719 81

And given that a man, who constantly evolving and can always learn any structure, the small business for him can be a mean to achieve any local goal. For example, when it comes to business in third distant countries where, for example, a man has not been before, and he wants to put some business matters for dissemination of eternal development technologies:
719 419 811

The structure of small business may have great advantages compared to other activities in terms of independence, which is important, and often a major factor in the eternal development technologies: **819 419 714**

One should strive to quickly help people in study of eternal development technologies through his/her own business: **914 819 87**

Creation of independent funding source of eternal development technology is also necessary:**518 491 617**

When doing business, it makes sense to develop self-organization. To become an organized person, you can use the number line: **419875 –** in order to be engaged in technologies of eternal development. In this case the numbers should be in your perception, as it were at a distance from you when generating an event, i.e., a line under which all the events you are busy with take place, such as of the current day and future, near or strategic. Thus, the numeric line correlation allows you to organize yourself and be organized person without taking unnecessary actions.

The Action Plan for the personal self-organization, developing the capacity of predictive control, can be used in the following series:
419 818 719 849.

Keep in mind that the concept of the eternal power of technology development is that a person can achieve any capacity. Naturally, one is able to do what is necessary for his eternal development, including the mastering of any business. A number for you to have the necessary knowledge and skills: **514918919**.

In technologies of eternal development, it is important that an event factor, not just the time often defines time, so there is need to use the number line: **914 41981**.

This number allows you to combine events and time. And in the future, when measuring, for example, some of your positions by events rather than time, such events as coming out of new successful large business after small business, you can immediately optimize your work just now. That is, what should you look for first, and to what you may not draw your attention at the beginning. For this there is a numerical series, optimizing choices:
419 814

All men are created by the God equal, and you with your actions also have almost equal chances. In this case, you can simply assume that at this point, you can know the subject matter more deeply. But, nevertheless, we must remember that others can learn it in the structure of eternal development. It means that the more and better you master the knowledge of the eternal, the more of the same opportunities may have others. Thus, the knowledge of eternal development has a high social value, and mastering them, you contribute to the eternal life of all people.

Assessment of knowledge aimed at eternal development in terms of increasing the knowledge in any area defined by the following number series: **418 718419 412**

Self-assessment and evaluation of others in technologies of the eternal development give a result in terms of common actions. To become a person about whom other people have a high regard for as a person capable of mastering the knowledge of eternal life, you must use the number line: **419 818719 914481.** This helps at the psychological level to take control of the team, for the other members of the staff and the community and as well to realize that it is possible to learn up to your level of knowledge of eternal life.

In eternal development technologies one must always be perfectly balanced at the level of solutions for a family in the whole, and therefore there are certain series of numbers, which, above all, creates the conditions for harmony among all family members, including the reaction of friends. Number is: **814 418 719**

In eternal development technologies the task is often determined by the need to achieve the mandatory result of the action, to settle the situation in any way. Classes and whatever hobbies have internal substructure constantly focused on the eternal development and acquisition of new forthcoming knowledge. One must properly focus the knowledge so that both the interests and activities of a particular deed were harmoniously linked in the common goal of eternal development: **718 419 47148**

Your business activity which allows you to help people to attain an eternal life, and, moreover, to implement particular technologies including very often unfamiliar ones at the early stages of social development towards eternity technology obviously is very useful for people what is deliberately understandable. Just a question is will it be expedient in the general economic connections. At this point it might be considered not only your focus, but also the objective economic realities which presented in the region and in the society as a whole: **419 718 814.**

When you say that your company is working for the purposes of implementation of eternal development technology, consider the following: the potential benefits of an enterprise engaged in perpetual development, are absolutely obvious, since they include many more factors of usual business and lay foundation for greater potential, greater reliability and sustainability. This is a must in order to allocate super profits and simple profit at a level of future development in technology of eternity exactly. Therefore, it is an advantage already. Next you should show naturally that the benefits may also be ideological. For example, work under the trademarks GRABOVOI ® or GRIGORIGRABOVOI ® suggests that the people working under this sign, at the same time support the ideology of eternal development, coupled with the eternal life of all the people according to the teachings of Gregory Grabovoi. In this way, you can show the benefits of its future enterprise including based on ideological grounds, which can be oriented towards the individual.

Your focus on the structure of the eternal development is such that you can offer a completely reliable products or better services and, in the sense of that the quality of service is defined by the focus on the eternal development. That is the case when a service is offered to a person the state of which is taken into account what directs him to perpetual development, therefore it provides a health and eternal development technologies' range, and also what develops business technologies itself: **51949871941**

There is a need for mandatory business sustainability for the purposes of eternal development, so many general trends in business technologies start to get a special meaning. The concept of beneficial use of benevolent case for technologies of eternal development is such that a chance in eternity is actually a system. One must understand that he has to intrinsically manage the fact that such situations, which will continuously develop his/her business, will be permanent: **814918712**. At the same time, he must actively manage the situation in this respect and he shall take all measures and means to achieve this: **819419417**

We should talk about the ability to use any, even the smallest, yet comfortable for your circumstances: **419 488 71**. When you consider the technology of eternal life in any circumstance, it appears that those circumstances start to evolve very rapidly and efficiently for you, showing gradually bigger prospects: **819 716**. Then the most important for you is to organize your own work, because always and often circumstances appear to be a lot good and favorable: **719 418 71**

There is nothing impossible in this world: **519 7148**. Especially if you do this for all peoples' eternal life, then accordingly you will be able to achieve what you set as your goal for the people and for yourself: **894 719 78 48**

498 719 418 series allow you to restore all that could be done, but often after other activities so you get method to control of the past by current events. Method of correcting of past events directly consists of the fact that you are to adjust the past events through the use of number series: **28914801890498.** Then, focusing on a number: **91431289** you get the adjusted result of past events in the present and future.

You must be able to use time: **814 418 81**. You can use the number line **418 41849**, which will assist in operations and often will initiate the action. Numerical series **4148188** helps at conversion of the time into money. You have to deal with money, so you can quickly learn how to convert. Accumulated knowledge can be practically applied to the conversion of time into eternal life. Realizing this, we can perceive technologically as the eternal past creates the future eternal life, which is irrespective towards the past. This suggests that life does not depend on money, but, as you can see, the money can be used as a kind of simulator, connected with reality, which allows developing of a methodology for eternal life. By analogy, one can identify a lot of other reality simulators that allow him/her to promptly learn the knowledge of eternal life, which is guaranteed to provide you and all other people healthy eternal life.

BUSINESS METHODS IN ETERNAL DEVELOPMENT

1. Business participants in eternal development can set the goal of ensuring eternal life, this provides a combination of events that contributes to the success of the business.

2. For business planning purposes, it is necessary to set eternal development in all areas of achievement of the goal. The features of such business planning may be multiple relationships in business development, which are better systematized by classes and directions. When new business areas arise, you can use standard systems for the eternal development of business management.

3. Form modern business by taking into account current achievements in society and the development of business management, applying forecasts correlated towards eternal development.

4. The organization of the eternal business planning process should be carried out in the presence of data on competitors, partners and sales markets. It is advisable to implement a standard plan for the transformation of competitive relations into partnership relations.

5. In the essence and significance of business planning for eternal development, it is necessary to consider the law of continuity in the inflows of material goods and intangible assets that ensure eternal life.

6. In the business of eternal development, it is important to associate the presentation of business plans with the history of the organization's business, which clearly reflects the organization's contribution to ensuring eternal life.

7. In case of eternal development, it is advisable to audit the business plan in such a way as to ensure eternal development with recommendations corresponding to the laws of eternal development or to establish a norm relating to eternal document circulation.

8. It is necessary to increase the role, practices and opportunities of business planning in the processes of achieving international business development.

9. Considering business as a system of relationships, it is necessary to find areas that create the next reality of eternal development.

10. In business planning functions, it is necessary to implement the principle of eternal development, which establishes eternally connected structures in business plans.

11. The peculiarities of drawing up business plans in the structures of eternal development are that the principle of eternal development of events should be taken into account in each event.

12. The principle of eternal development in business should be implemented, which is that over time similar levels of management can be obtained from various documents.

13. When implementing eternal development, it follows from the principle of eternal life for everyone to obtain business technologies in all areas of business.

14. Methods of forecasting profits and losses should be related both by direct receipt of information about events based on the development of spiritual abilities and by the generalization of information at different intervals.

15. In the development of business characteristics, it is necessary to lay eternal connections both between internal business technology systems and between external ones, including prognosticated events.

16. When analyzing the business environment of the organization, it is necessary to take into account the coefficient of mutual influence of business systems on ensuring the goal of eternal development.

17. The marketing plan should include the development of the properties of eternity emanating from goods.

18. The production plan should include measures that ensure the eternal life of business process participants.

19. Through the organizational plan, implement the business principle of eternal development, which states that greater intersection of events of eternal life will create significantly greater consequences that ensure eternal life.

20. Enter into the financial plan funds specifically designed to ensure eternal life.

21. In risk assessment, use the principle of natural risk reduction when implementing eternal development.

22. Apply business organization techniques that combine spiritual management of reality with specific practice.

23. When drawing up any plans in business, proceed from the practice of eternity of a person who has knowledge of eternal development.

24. Use all possible achievements of science, technology and spiritual technologies of eternal development to develop your business.

25. In the output of the business plan, show the logic of developing business processes that ensure eternal life.

26. Implement the principle of universality of business laws of eternal development.

27. When providing business data, report on the possibility of their use for the development of other areas of entrepreneurial activity.

28. In product information, explicitly or indirectly include an information that allows you to use this product or its combination with other products in ensuring eternal development.

29. When conducting economic research for business development, first of all identify for possible development those areas that have more significant signs of eternal development.

30. Adhere to the principle of structuring areas of activity in the market, in which activities saturated with technologies of eternal development should contribute to the saturation of technologies of eternal development of all other areas of the market.

31. Try to summarize information coming from different systems of the market economy to objectify the achievements of eternal development through business technologies.

32. Develop the abilities of yourself and other people to ensure eternal life in any creative way.

33. Combine different markets by implementing the idea of eternal development.

34. Assess the business situation not only economically, but also with the results of spiritual development that ensures eternal life for everyone. Intensively develop one-temporary educational courses and technologies in a business environment that allow you to get a general and spiritual education that provides students and all other people with eternal life.

35. Use the experience of implementing eternal development, transferring it to other business structures.

36. Create the sustainability of enterprises of eternal development in the market by fully taking into account all market information, including data from forecast management technologies.

37. Manage the predicted situation in advance, focusing on the goal of ensuring eternal development.

38. Use implemented projects that ensure eternal development as template systems.

39. Attract well-known ways of selling goods and develop new ones that ensure eternal development.

40. At any level of business activity, always ensure eternal life for yourself and everyone else.

41. Ensure an increase in eternal development technologies with an increase in the operating time of your business.

42. Produce the sale of goods in such a way that the goods sold contribute to the sale of the next product, ensuring eternal development.

43. Inform about business that ensures eternal development without restrictions, as ensuring the eternal life of each person is always legal, meets all moral and moral social principles.

44. Implement eternal development through business technologies systematically, perform what is planned in accordance with the set time.

45. Detail business schemes to such a level as to take into account all the elements that allow you to most effectively ensure eternal life.

46. Identify data proving that your business contributes to the process of ensuring the eternal life of everyone, and on the basis of this, involve third parties in cooperation. 47. In accordance with the law of universal eternal development, constantly increase the sales of goods and intellectual products.

48. Have time to increase the potential of your business to sell necessary products that ensure eternal life.

49. Widely apply dynamic self-recovering systems that allow you to implement a business of eternal development.

50. Develop business links in such a way as to more effectively apply the principle of mutual influence of each link of business and external systems in eternal development.

51. Always prioritize guaranteed ensuring the eternal life of business participants and at the same time all others in any projects.

52. Carry out activities in accordance with the law of mandatory access of eternal life technologies to each person.

53. Regularly apply spiritual predictive management methods along with economic methods to obtain optimal data that ensures eternal development.

54. Use the combination of different spheres and objects of business processes in increasing resources that provide eternal development.

55. Keep the necessary amount of funds to ensure eternal development.

Made in the USA
Columbia, SC
06 December 2023

27880045R00098